LIFE Year in Pictures

The Year in Pictures 1999

EDITOR Killian Jordan
PICTURE EDITOR Azurea Lee Dudley
ART DIRECTOR Bob Villaflor
ASSISTANT ART DIRECTOR Kim Kowalski
ASSOCIATE PICTURE EDITOR Donna Aceto
ASSISTANT PICTURE EDITOR Dot McMahon
PHOTO RESEARCH Lauren Steel
WRITER Jenny Allen
CONTRIBUTOR Gerard Wright
CHIEF OF REPORTERS Deirdre Van Dyk
REPORTERS Kathy Chu, Akiko Ichikawa, Nick Lansing
DESIGN CONSULTANT Neal Boulton
COPY CHIEF Kathleen Berger
And all members of
the LIFE Copy Department

Time Inc. Home Entertainment

PRESIDENT Stuart Hotchkiss
EXECUTIVE DIRECTOR, BRANDED BUSINESSES David Arfine
EXECUTIVE DIRECTOR, NON BRANDED BUSINESSES Alicia Longobardo
DIRECTOR, BRAND LICENSING Risa Turken
DIRECTOR, MARKETING SERVICES Michael Barrett
DIRECTOR, RETAIL & SPECIAL SALES Tom Mifsud
ASSOCIATE DIRECTORS Roberta Harris, Kenneth Maehlum
PRODUCT MANAGERS Andre Okolowitz, Niki Viswanathan, Daria Raehse
ASSOCIATE PRODUCT MANAGERS Dennis Sheehan, Meredith Shelley, Bill Totten, Lauren Zaslansky
ASSISTANT PRODUCT MANAGERS Victoria Alfonso, Jennifer Dowell, Ann Gillespie
ASSOCIATE LICENSING MANAGER Regina Feiler
EDITORIAL OPERATIONS DIRECTOR John Calvano
BOOK PRODUCTION MANAGER Jessica McGrath
ASSISTANT BOOK PRODUCTION MANAGER Jonathan Polsky
BOOK PRODUCTION COORDINATOR Kristen Lizzi
FULFILLMENT MANAGER Richard Perez
ASSISTANT FULFILLMENT MANAGER Tara Schimming
FINANCIAL DIRECTOR Tricia Griffin
FINANCIAL MANAGER Robert Dente
ASSOCIATE FINANCIAL MANAGER Steven Sandonato
EXECUTIVE ASSISTANT Mary Jane Rigoroso
SPECIAL THANKS TO Emily Rabin, Jennifer Bomhoff

COVER PHOTOGRAPHS
Front
The Kennedys: Filippo Monteforte/Olympia-Sipa Press
Balloon: Patrick Durand/Corbis Sygma
Soccer: Hector Mata/Agence France Presse
Back
Roberto Benigni: Eric Draper/Associated Press
Softcover edition
Eclipse: Sylvain Estibal/Agence France Presse
Cow: Caroline Minjolle/Lookat Photos

Copyright 2000
Time Inc. Home Entertainment

Published by

Books

Time Inc.
1271 Avenue of the Americas
New York, New York 10020

First Edition

ISSN: 1092-0463
ISBN: 1-883013-87-9

"LIFE" is a trademark of Time Inc.

We welcome your comments and suggestions about LIFE Books. Please write to us at:

LIFE Books
Attention: Book Editors
PO Box 11016
Des Moines, IA 50336-1016

If you would like to order any of our hardcover Collector's Edition books, please call us at 1-800-327-6388 (Monday through Friday, 7:00 a.m.— 8:00 p.m. or Saturday, 7:00 a.m.— 6:00 p.m. Central Time).

PRINTED IN THE UNITED STATES OF AMERICA

The 1999 Album

6   Winter January February March
28   1st Quarter Report
34   Latin Sizzlers

40   Spring April May June
64   2nd Quarter Report
70   You Go, Girls!

76   Summer July August September
102   3rd Quarter Report
108   The Comeback Kid

114   Fall October November December
132   4th Quarter Report

138   Remembering

159   Index

Collapsing after a trek across the mountains into Macedonia, a Kosovar refugee is swarmed by news photographers.

Contents

Snow Day!

Ah, the San Joaquin Valley! Land of orange groves, of sunny vineyards, of . . . snow? In late January, residents of this fertile Southern California basin woke to the area's first measurable snow in almost 25 years. The six-inch fall caused some chaos, including a 40-mile shutdown of Interstate 5, the state's main north-south artery. But most people, like this family in Bakersfield, couldn't get enough of it.

Winter

Jan. 1 The euro, the European Union's new **unified currency,** debuts to wide public indifference in 11 countries.

Jan. 5 The U.S. Agriculture Department agrees to pay some $300 million to **settle a lawsuit** brought by 1,000 African American farmers who had accused the government of racial bias in denying them loans and subsidies since the early 1980s.

Jan. 6 Illinois Republican Dennis Hastert is sworn in as **speaker of the House,** succeeding Newt Gingrich, who had abruptly resigned in November at the request of GOP colleagues. Interim speaker-designate Robert Livingston (R-La.) was also forced out after *Hustler* publisher Larry Flynt threatened to air details of his marital infidelity.

Jan. 7 Chief Justice William H. Rehnquist formally opens President Clinton's Senate **impeachment trial,** the first in 131 years. The President faces charges of perjury and obstruction of justice stemming from attempts to cover up a relationship with former White House intern Monica Lewinsky.

Sudden Death

At one o'clock on a sunny January 26, most of central Colombia's inhabitants were enjoying their lunch breaks. Then the earth shuddered. In 30 seconds a magnitude-six earthquake had ravaged four provinces. Landslides and collapsing buildings killed nearly 1,000, injured some 4,000 others and left 200,000 homeless. Using their hands, rescue workers dug through rubble for survivors, including this man. In the hard-hit city of Armenia, a makeshift morgue was created in a soccer stadium—the only location big enough to hold the hundreds of corpses.

Jan. 15 Faced with 22,000 empty slots (6 percent of its active-duty force), the U.S. Navy announces that it will lower educational requirements to **spur enlistment.** Only 90 percent of new recruits must have high school diplomas, down from 95 percent.

Jan. 22 The Defense Department announces that 1,145 military personnel were discharged in 1998 for being gay. Oddly, the figure has risen each year since the Clinton administration instituted a **"don't ask, don't tell"** policy designed to reduce the number fired for their sexual orientation.

Jan. 22 Although in fragile health, **Pope John Paul II** commences the 85th foreign tour of his papacy. After a five-day sojourn in Mexico, he will visit the United States.

Jan. 28 In history's second-largest **automotive deal,** Ford Motor Co. agrees to buy Volvo Cars for $6.45 billion. Last year's Daimler-Chrysler merger was valued at $38 billion.

What a Mess

On February 3, a cargoless 639-foot Japanese-operated freighter dropped anchor off the southern Oregon shore. Overnight, rough weather—high winds and 25-foot waves—drove the *New Carissa* aground. Badly battered, the ship began oozing oil. A Navy team then dropped a napalm mixture onboard, hoping the 400,000 gallons of fuel would burn off quickly. But only half the fuel was aflame when the ship ripped apart—the stern was stuck in the sand; the bow lay half submerged nearby. A tug pulled the bow out to sea, where a torpedo finally sank it. As months went by and cleanup costs hit $30 million, the stern still hadn't been fully dismantled, and oil was still washing ashore.

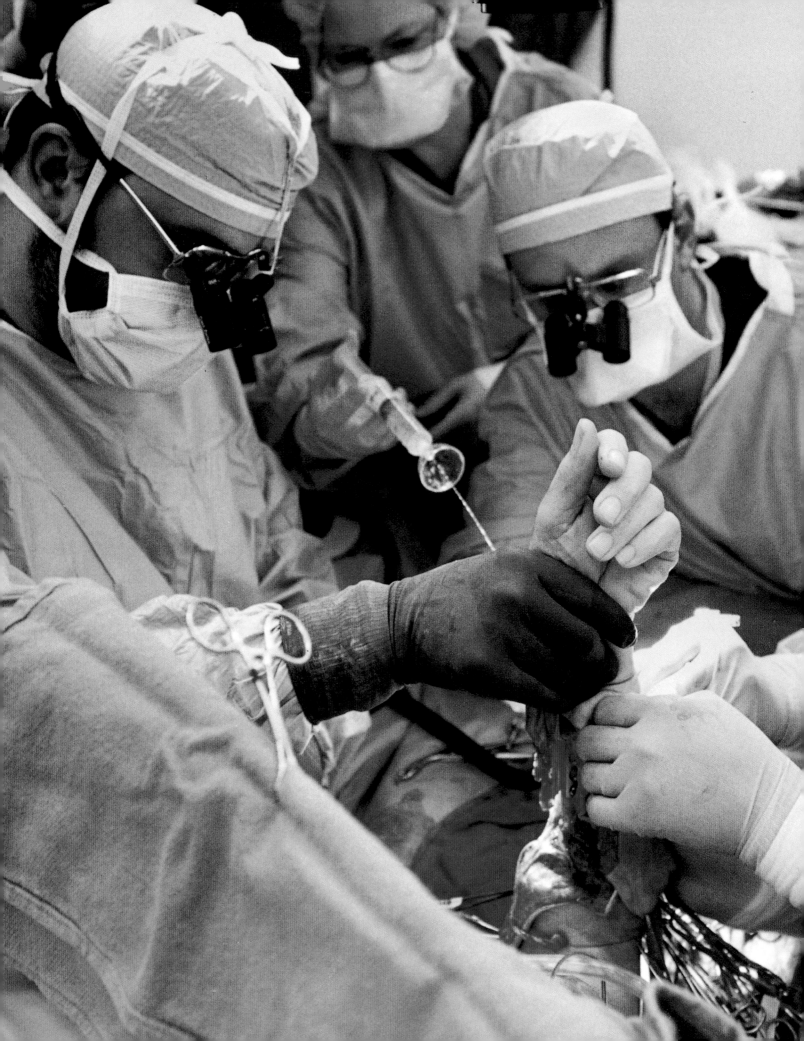

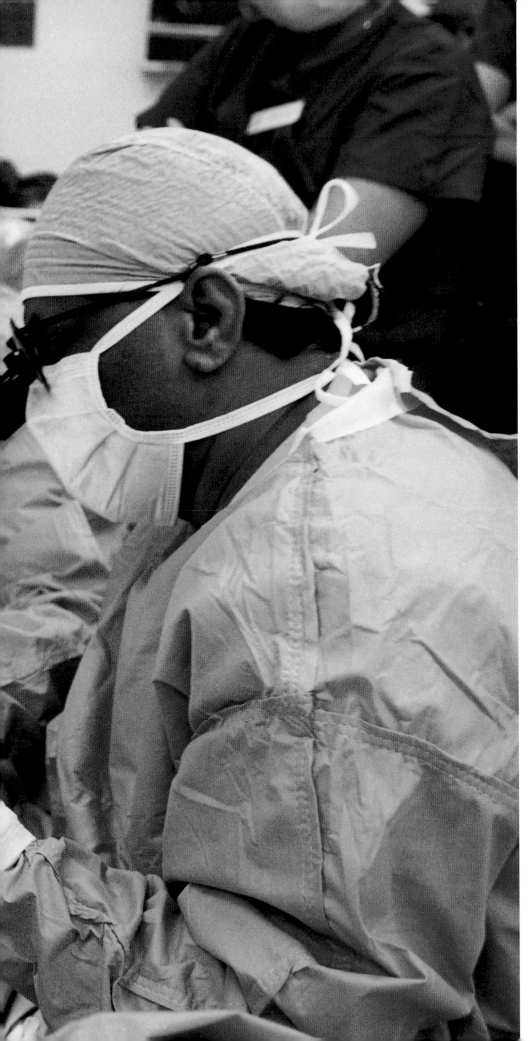

Feb. 4 Four plainclothes New York City police officers allegedly **fire 41 shots** at Amadou Diallo, an unarmed West African immigrant, striking him 19 times. Two months later, all four will be indicted on second-degree murder charges.

Feb. 5 The National Basketball Association opens its 53rd season with a shortened **50-game schedule.** The delayed opener follows a 204-day player lockout.

Feb. 9 Dartmouth College announces the end of its 150-year tradition of single-sex fraternities and sororities. Officials at the Ivy League school, which inspired the movie *Animal House,* believe that **the Greek system** fostered binge drinking and social stratification.

Feb. 12 After a five-week trial, the U.S. Senate **acquits President Bill Clinton** of impeachment charges arising from his relationship with a White House intern. Clinton tells the nation he is "profoundly sorry" for his actions.

Hand to Hand
The cadaver's hand may look gruesome, but consider: In January, a team of 17 doctors and nurses at Jewish Hospital in Louisville, Ky., attached the hand of an anonymous donor (later identified as a convicted murderer who had taken his own life) to the wrist of Matthew Scott, a 37-year-old paramedic who lost his dominant left hand 14 years ago. Scott's is the first American hand transplant; only four months earlier, French surgeons had performed successful surgery on a New Zealander. By October, Scott reported that he could butter a bagel, hold a phone and, best of all, "hug people with both arms."

Shared Sorrow

For three days after King Hussein's February funeral, his widow welcomed thousands of ordinary women into the palace in Amman. Hussein's passionate peacekeeping in the Middle East earned the respect of world leaders; to Jordanians, Hussein was their beloved monarch. Queen Noor has refused to discuss the intrigue behind the king's startling eleventh-hour decision to remove his brother from the line of succession in favor of Abdullah, his son from a previous marriage—who in turn named Noor's son Hamzah, 18, crown prince. But she has spoken eloquently of her husband's courageous battle against the cancer that took his life at 63 and of her abiding devotion. "I start my days talking to him. I end my days talking to him."

Feb. 13 American Airlines pilots **holding a sickout** are fined $10 million for violating a return-to-work order issued three days earlier. The labor dispute canceled thousands of flights and tore a $225 million chunk out of the company's first-quarter earnings.

Feb. 25 A jury in Jasper County, Tex., sentences 24-year-old John William King to **death by lethal injection.** The first to stand trial, King is one of three white men who are charged with chaining James Byrd Jr., a 49-year-old black man, to the back of a truck last year and dragging him three miles to his death.

Feb. 27 Nigerian voters overwhelmingly elect **their former military dictator,** retired general Olusegun Obasanjo, to the presidency of Africa's most populous nation.

Mar. 1 Angered by American and British support for Rwanda's Tutsi-led government, Rwandan Hutu rebels **kidnap and kill** eight foreign tourists, including an Oregon couple, in a Ugandan national park on the border of the Democratic Republic of Congo.

Snow Zone

On February 21 a sudden snowslide smothered the Swiss alpine village of Evolene, killing 12. Over four weeks, hundreds of other avalanches, triggered by record-breaking snowfalls, thundered through the Alps. Worst hit was the Austrian resort of Galtür, where villagers and tourists dug at the compacted masses with hands and shovels, freeing some buried victims; 31 others did not survive. By the time the slides stopped, nearly 100 people had been killed in four countries.

Mar. 4 Capt. Richard J. Ashby, the Marine pilot whose plane **severed a ski-gondola cable** in an Italian resort last year—an accident that left 20 dead—is acquitted of involuntary manslaughter by an American military jury. He will later be found guilty of obstruction of justice—for destroying a videotape record of the flight.

Mar. 8 A Taiwanese-born scientist is fired for **security breaches** at the Los Alamos National Laboratory in New Mexico. Officials suspect Wen Ho Lee leaked secrets that allowed China to develop advanced nuclear weapons.

Mar. 12 One month before marking its 50th anniversary—and on the eve of its first involvement in a war—the North Atlantic Treaty Organization **welcomes three new members.** The Czech Republic, Hungary and Poland represent NATO's first expansion since 1982 and are the first countries of the Soviet-allied Warsaw Pact to gain entry.

That Face

Seventy million viewers—including this Toronto electronics store employee— couldn't resist watching Barbara Walters's March interview with Monica Lewinsky. They saw a young woman struggling to appear mature, . . . but did she really feel that giving Clinton a peek at her thong panties was a "small, subtle, flirtatious gesture"? Vixen? Maybe. Or maybe Maine's Sen. Susan Collins got it right, after seeing Lewinsky's taped deposition: "All I can say is that I found her heartbreakingly young."

Mar. 16 All 20 members of the European Union's executive branch, the European Commission, **tender their resignations** after a report accuses them of corruption and financial mismanagement.

Mar. 17 The International Olympic Committee expels six members who have been implicated in **ethical violations** (principally, receiving cash gifts and other favors) in Salt Lake City's successful campaign to host the 2002 Winter Olympics.

Mar. 17 Gaby Vernoff, of Los Angeles, delivers a baby girl after having been artificially inseminated with sperm extracted from her husband 30 hours **after his death** and frozen for three years. "She's your average healthy kid," one of Vernoff's doctors says of the infant, "born by the hand of God and the hand of man—but a little more man than usual."

Terror in the Night

Amtrak's *City of New Orleans* pulled out of Chicago shortly after eight p.m. on March 15, bound for Louisiana. An hour and a half later, the 14-car train was rolling quietly through the countryside when it rammed the rear of a tractor-trailer at a crossing. Eleven cars were derailed; one engine sheared the sleeper in two, killing 11 passengers, including three children. One hundred twenty-two other passengers were injured. The truck's driver, who was unhurt, said the crossing lights didn't flash until he was already on the tracks. At year's end, investigators had been unable to confirm his account.

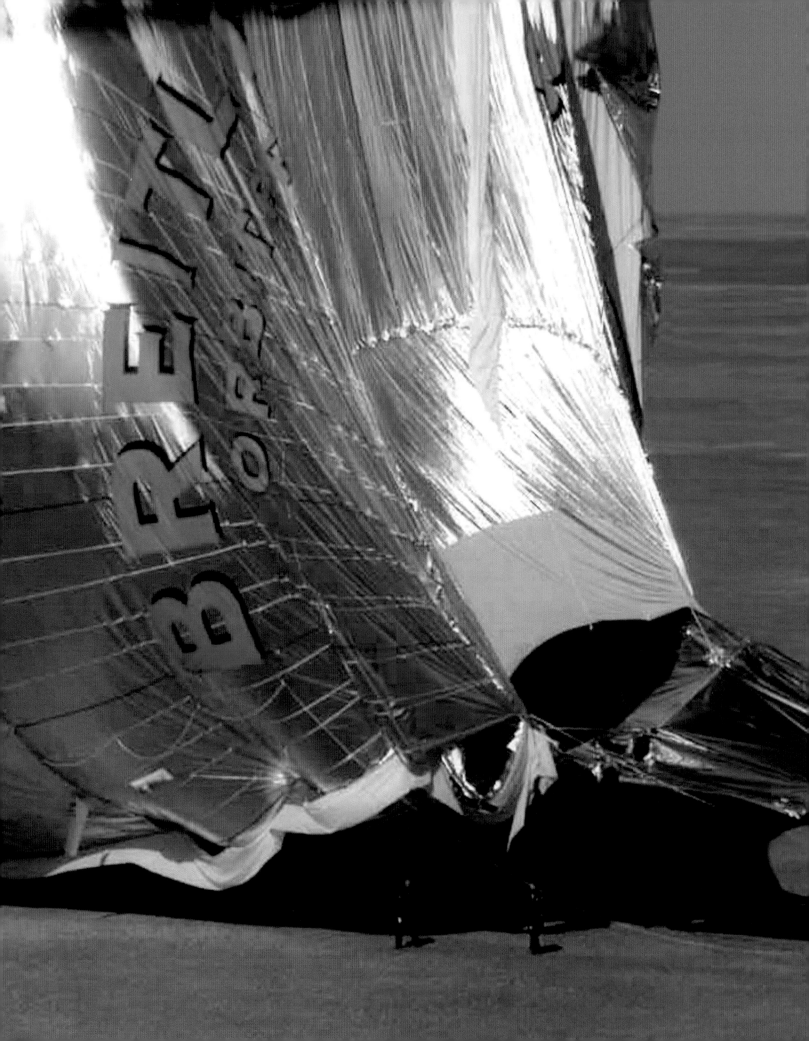

Mar. 24 In the wake of continued Serbian aggression against ethnic Albanian residents of the province of Kosovo, the North Atlantic Treaty Organization **launches air strikes** against Serbia. Four days earlier, intensifying violence had forced international cease-fire monitors to leave Kosovo.

Mar. 26 Dr. Jack Kevorkian, a longtime advocate and enabler of **assisted suicide**, is convicted in Michigan of second-degree murder for killing a terminally ill man by lethal injection. He will later be sentenced to 10 to 25 years in prison.

Mar. 27 NATO forces successfully execute a **daring helicopter rescue** of the American pilot of a downed U.S. F-117 stealth fighter six hours after the aircraft is shot down by Serbian forces some 35 miles from Belgrade.

Once Over Lightly

True, it came outfitted with satellite telephones and a fax machine, but you couldn't actually *steer* it. Brian Jones, 51, and Bertrand Piccard, 41, had to artfully latch on to powerful jet streams to make the 180-foot-high *Breitling Orbiter 3* the first hot-air balloon to float around the globe nonstop. Nineteen days after takeoff in Switzerland, *Orbiter* touched down safely in the Egyptian desert. By long-distance balloonist standards, the journey was uneventful—just a four-day loss of contact with mission control and a dwindling supply of fuel. Said an ecstatic Piccard, "It was beautiful."

Victory from the Sky

On the afternoon of March 24, President Clinton was told that U.S. envoy Richard Holbrooke's last-ditch mission to Belgrade—to end Yugoslav President Slobodan Milosevic's war on ethnic Albanians—had been a bust. "Let's do it," said Clinton. Two hours later, NATO bombs shook Pristina, Kosovo's capital city. Over the next 11 weeks, 10,000 Serbian troops were killed or injured, and roads, railways, and government buildings were destroyed. The strategy worked: Milosevic, who many believed would not cave without the threat of ground troops, surrendered in 78 days.

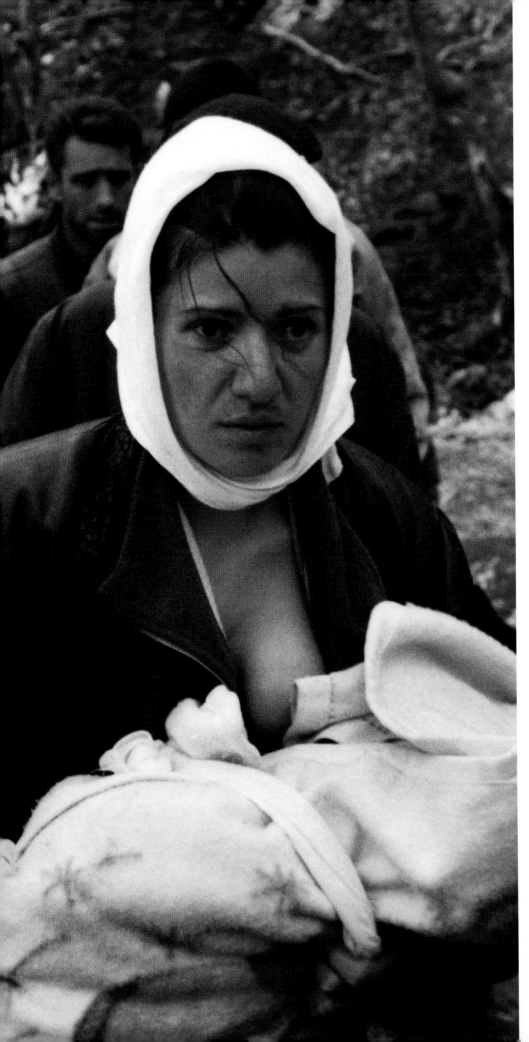

Mar. 28 Underdog Purdue scores a 62–45 victory over Duke, becoming the first Big Ten team to win the **NCAA women's basketball** championship.

Mar. 29 The Dow-Jones industrial average **closes above 10,000** for the first time in its history, at 10,006.78. It had opened 1999 at 9,212.8.

Mar. 29 The University of Connecticut edges Duke, 77–74, for the **NCAA men's basketball** championship.

Mar. 30 An Oregon jury awards a total of **$81 million in damages** (later reduced to $32 million by a judge) to the family of a deceased smoker. It is the largest sum ever awarded to a single plaintiff in a smoking-related suit.

Forced to Flee

The Serbs had torched their houses, executed their loved ones, looted their towns and cities, all to roust them from Kosovo. A week after NATO bombing began on March 24, some 300,000 ethnic Albanians had made their way to neighboring Albania, Montenegro and Macedonia. Some had been herded by Serbs into boxcars, some came by tractor, some trudged on foot. At Blace, the Macedonian border crossing, up to 60,000 refugees, including this nursing mother, spent a cold night outdoors before United Nations officials persuaded the government to let them pass. They were among the so-called fortunate: One train had been turned back at Blace, its 1,000 passengers returned to hell.

So rare . . .

A blue moon is the second full moon in a single month, something that occurs only once in a . . . long time. Double the rarity this year: In '99 we saw *two* blue moons, on January 31 and March 31. Missed them? They'll double up again in 2018.

A tip of the hat to . . .

Dolly, the cloned sheep who produced three—all natural—lamblets in March. Their papa is David, a Welsh mountain ram.

"I like Bill Clinton. Do I think he's a total idiot? Yes."

Former White House staffer Harold Ickes

"The President's conduct is boorish, indefensible, even reprehensible. It does not threaten the Republic."

Sen. Richard Bryan (D-Nev.), on the impeachment proceedings

THE POWER OF PINK

The color of the year turned up on Shakespeare's (and Oscar's) love, Gwyneth Paltrow.

Meet the press

The first joint appearance of Britain's Prince Charles and his longtime Other Woman, Camilla Parker Bowles, was billed by one London paper as "Meet the Mistress." This brief glimpse was part of the prince's campaign to normalize the formerly illicit relationship. After all, he'd like to bring her home to Mother.

IRISH IMMIGRATION 33 USA

Welcome home

It's not just the McCourts: The Irish have poured into America at such a rate that 15 percent of Americans now claim Irish ancestry. The Postal Service commemorates the voyagers with this new offering.

Barbie, blue?

Not, perhaps, her very *best* year (sales growth has slowed dramatically), but this one-of-a-kind Barbie kept her chin up and her diamonds ($70,000 worth) sparkly to face her 40th anniversary with the usual aplomb. No midlife crisis for her!

"If you ever think you're too small to be effective, you've never been in bed with a mosquito."

Wendy Schaetzel Lesko, head of a group that encourages kids to get involved in politics

"This is not about the Second Amendment. This is about parents burying their children."

Suzann Wilson, mother of an 11-year-old girl killed in the Jonesboro, Ark., school shootings, chastising gun-rights advocates

"See what happens when you let men into the Cabinet?"

Secretary of State Madeleine Albright, on two male colleagues who were talking about clothes shopping

"One third of the children today are born into homes without families."

Former Vice President Dan Quayle, as quoted in a book published this year

"It's not as exciting as a case I had on *The People's Court* involving a python that swallowed a Chihuahua."

TV judge and former New York City Mayor Ed Koch, on the impeachment trial

The diva department

"No nonsense" doesn't begin to describe TV (and former family court) **Judge Judy Sheindlin.** Daytime's queen of the courthouse said it best with her own book title: *Don't Pee on My Leg and Tell Me It's Raining.* And then she beat out her husband in the ratings.

Former Fugee **Lauryn Hill** doo-wopped her way to a record-breaking five major Grammys on the big night—including Best New Artist and Album of the Year for *The Miseducation of Lauryn Hill.*

FLASHBACK: TURN OF TWO CENTURIES

	1899	1999
Average life expectancy of an American (in years)	47.3	76.7
The death rate for children under a year old (per thousand)	162	7

Tails, you win

New quarters are being rolled out by the U.S. Mint, one for each state, in the order of its ratification of the Constitution or inception of statehood. In 2000, we'll have a new Sacagawea dollar coin.

Well, I declare

There's a presidential election right around the corner. Early in '99, the campaign included these candidates:
**Lamar Alexander
Elizabeth Dole
Bill Bradley
Gov. George W. Bush (R-Tex.)
Steve Forbes
Al Gore
Sen. John McCain (R-Ariz.)
Dan Quayle
Sen. Robert C. Smith (R-N.H.)**

Let's meet at my house Sunday before the game.

–God

You might want to pay attention

The campaign to get people thinking about God began in Florida, then spread across the U.S. Initially financed by an anonymous donor, the messages are direct—but charmingly quirky.

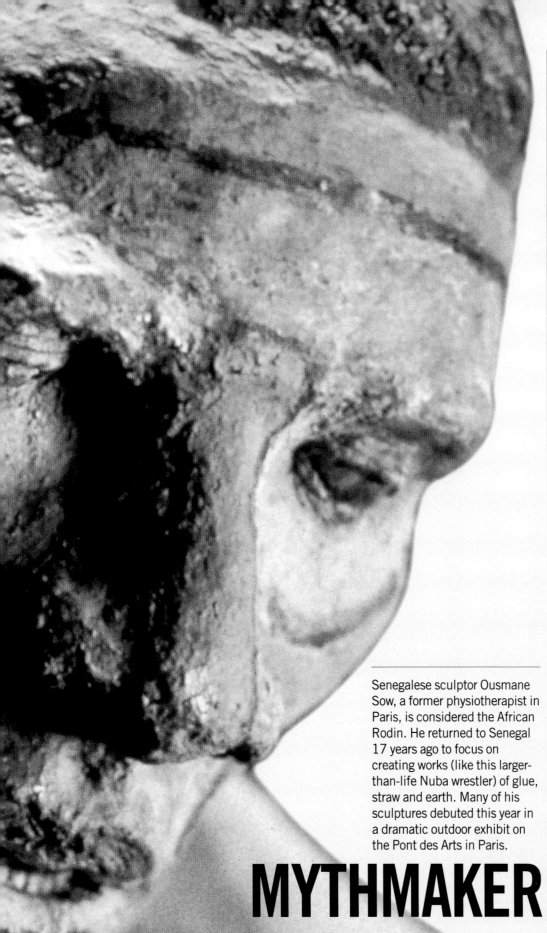

Like your wrestling on wheels? Body slams, hugely popular in the '50s and '60s, made a comeback on TNN's *RollerJam*. Skaters like "Sisters of Suffering" and "The Barracuda" go for the gold.

"You missin' Billy just about now, ain'tcha?"

Oscar emcee Whoopi Goldberg, whose jokes were notably crude, referring to 1998's host, Billy Crystal

Most happy fella

The Italian actor-director Roberto Benigni, elated by his two Oscars, promised to "make love to everybody."

Senegalese sculptor Ousmane Sow, a former physiotherapist in Paris, is considered the African Rodin. He returned to Senegal 17 years ago to focus on creating works (like this larger-than-life Nuba wrestler) of glue, straw and earth. Many of his sculptures debuted this year in a dramatic outdoor exhibit on the Pont des Arts in Paris.

MYTHMAKER

FOUR FOR THE AGES

These forces of nature took themselves out of the game in 1999, and the loss is all ours. **Michael Jordan** was first, announcing his retirement—for real this time—in January. Then the Great One, **Wayne Gretzky**, bowed out as gracefully as he had skated during his 20 magical, record-studded years in the National Hockey League. With 148 victories behind him, Denver Broncos quarterback **John Elway** scooped up another Super Bowl ring and headed home. And **Steffi Graf**, an amazing 22 Grand Slam tournament titles in hand, also rode off into the sunset.

"He's the truth, the whole truth, and nothing but the truth."

Former Chicago Bulls forward Sidney Green

WAYNE GRETZKY

STEFFI GRAF

JOHN ELWAY

MICHAEL JORDAN

Intensely competitive and transcendentally accomplished, Jordan *owned* the NBA during his reign: six titles, five MVP awards, 10 scoring titles. That's why Larry Bird said, "I think he's God disguised as Michael Jordan."

Martinmania

Ever since Ricky Martin shook it at the Grammy ceremonies, "I've been living, literally, *la vida loca*—the crazy life," he says, referring to the title of his ubiquitous hit song. The eponymous English debut album of the former star of *General Hospital* and Puerto Rican pop group Menudo sold 660,000 copies in its first week of release.

Latin Sizzlers

Tight clothes, hot lights and thundering rhythms—February's 41st Annual Grammy Awards had all the elements of a night to remember. So why was it turning into such a crashing bore? No disrespect to Lauryn Hill, Celine Dion, Madonna and other winners; but as those familiar stars filed up and down the stage collecting their awards, a heavy sense of predictability settled over L.A.'s Shrine Auditorium. You could almost hear the Armani-clad bottoms shifting in their seats. And then, from out of nowhere, a 27-year-old Puerto Rican Adonis named Ricky Martin appeared onstage, belting out a Spanish song called "La Copa de la Vida" and whipping the most supercharged pelvis America had seen since the King himself. It was more than a performance, it was an explosion, a Latin explosion that left viewers across America gasping for air, scratching their heads. "Ricky Martin—is he a cutie or what?" said Grammy host Rosie O'Donnell. "I never heard of him before."

Americans now spend as much on salsa as they do on ketchup.

She has now—everyone has. By June, when he played outside the *Today* show in Manhattan, crowds of screeching fans grew so thick that people who worked nearby needed special detour maps to get to their offices. And to many, Martin is much more than just the crooner-of-the-month—he is a harbinger of America's Latinized future.

Over the last 50 years, the nation's Hispanic population has risen from 1.5 percent to 12 percent, or 30 million, and Latin influence pervades everything from baseball to business. By autumn, not only had Martin's debut album sold five million copies, but four additional Latin artists had albums in pop's Top 40: Christina Aguilera, Marc Anthony, Santana and Jennifer Lopez. "Hispanics," proclaimed *Newsweek,* "are hip, hot and making history."

Which is precisely the kind of statement that makes many Latinos laugh—or squirm. Twenty years ago, many people thought that the 1980s would be the Decade of the Hispanic. Apparently, says Christy Haubegger, publisher of *Latina* magazine, "our decade was postponed." Does a flash flood of Latin-based pop music really signal a newfound respect for Latin culture—or does it just mean we'll be seeing more TV commercials featuring talking Chihuahuas? "We need to decide exactly what this 'Latin Explosion' is celebrating," says actress Daisy Fuentes. "That Ricky Martin shakes his ass really well? Or that Latin people have a great culture?"

Both, actually. Many Ricky Martin fans are interested in far more than his glutes. Take Debbie Duncan of Shawnee Mission, Kans. "When I first heard 'Livin' la Vida Loca,' I instantly went out and bought a Spanish dictionary and CD-ROM," she says. "I'm also reading anything I can find about Puerto Rico." Cindy Novak of Omaha has made a point of "learning more about Latin culture" and has even "taken up Latin dancing. Salsa and the merengue are great for exercise." After waiting in line for six hours, Bridget McMahon of Longmeadow, Mass., "actually met Ricky," who was "quite surprised that I spoke Spanish—he gave me a thumbs-up, something that I will never forget. What I most admire about Ricky is

Young, Gifted and Hot
Ricky Martin's (top) musical taste ran to bands like Cheap Trick and Boston until his mother "grabbed me by the ear and took me to see Celia Cruz and Tito Puente." Says actress Daisy Fuentes (above): "Most of us are very Americanized. But we bring to the table a special sense of flavor and passion."

Mix Master

Marc Anthony, the new king of salsa music, had a uniquely American upbringing in New York City. On the streets of Spanish Harlem, he once said, he would hear Panamanian Rubén Blades and disco diva Gloria Gaynor blasting from apartment windows, and rockers like the Doobie Brothers playing on car radios. His newest album, out this year, blends these influences—and many others.

THE TRAILBLAZERS

1. CORBIS/PENGUIN 2. SUZIE BLEEDEN/GLOBE 3. PHOTOFEST 4. MOMA FILM STILLS ARCHIVE/UA 5. CORBIS/BETTMANN-UPI 6. MARC BRYAN-BROWN/CORBIS OUTLINE 7. CATARINA/STILLS/RETNA 8. TOM HUTCHINS/SPORTS ILLUSTRATED 9. LISA ROSE/GLOBE

Today's Latin superstars follow a luminous line of entertainment and sports superachievers, including: 1. bandleader, comedian and Lucy-lover Desi Arnaz; 2. Spanish crooner Julio Iglesias, whose sons Enrique and Julio Jr. are following in his footsteps; 3. Broadway legend Chita Rivera; 4. Oscar-winning actress Rita Moreno; 5. Hall-of-Famer Roberto Clemente; 6. guitar virtuoso Carlos Santana, whose recent *Supernatural* has sold over three million copies; 7. Celia Cruz, the undisputed queen of Latin music; 8. Pancho Gonzales, the world's best tennis player in the 1950s; 9. Tito Puente, King of the Mambo.

MICHAEL CAULFIELD/AP

In a few decades, experts say, one American in four will be of Latin origin.

that he can express himself clearly in many languages and is able to unite the world through music."

The significance of these remarks can be summed up in one word: respect. In the past, however much white Americans cheered Celia Cruz, Desi Arnaz or Roberto Clemente, few showed much interest in where they came from. But now, "Americans are becoming more comfortable, not only with Spanish, but with the whole idea of a multicultural society," says Angelo Figueroa, managing editor of *People en Español*. Ricky Martin's fans will tell you that behind each irresistible Latin rhythm, each savory Latin cuisine, each eye-popping Latin style, there are slews of cultures, from more than 20 different countries, of infinite richness. And that's why Karen Rosas, a Ricky-worshiper from Orlando, has this request: "It's wonderful that Latin culture is finally getting its fair share of attention in America," she says. "But, please, don't call it a Latin explosion. Latin America didn't just 'explode' overnight. It's always been here." And now we know it's here to stay.

Out of Sight

The most surprising pop star of 1999 was Jennifer Lopez, an actress known for her breakthrough role in *Selena,* a movie tribute to the young Tejano singing sensation Selena Quintanilla Perez. She lip-synched her way through *Selena,* so few in the music business suspected she could sing—until her debut album, *On the 6,* sold 1.5 million copies.

Living with Loss

Jessica Holliday huddled under one table, Diwata Perez and Lauren Townsend under another, as Dylan Klebold and Eric Harris blasted away in the Columbine (Colo.) High School library. When the shooters moved on, some students were able to flee. Outside, Jessica (left) asked Diwata (right) about Lauren, her best friend. "Her eyes were closed," said Diwata. "Maybe she passed out." Jessica feared worse, and offered an anguished prayer. "I was saying, 'Oh, God, please tell me there's some hope.'" Months after the rampage, she says of Lauren's death, "I haven't been able to accept it."

Spring

Apr. 1 Ending a quarter century of Inuit land claims, **Canada creates Nunavut,** a 770,000-square-mile territory with the same powers and responsibilities as the Northwest Territories (from which it was carved) and the Yukon. The Inuit, who make up 85 percent of Nunavut's 27,000 citizens, gain full control of one sixth of the land and leadership in the 19-member legislature.

Apr. 2 A 30-year-old technology consultant from New Jersey is arrested for creating **the most infectious computer virus** ever. In three days, "Melissa" created glitches in more than 100,000 computers. Among the victims: Boeing, Lockheed Martin and the U.S. Marine Corps.

Apr. 4 For the first time, major league baseball's **season opener** takes place in Mexico. The Colorado Rockies beat the San Diego Padres, 8–2, at Estadio Monterrey.

Up in Smoke

Floridians dreaded a reprise. The worst wildfires in the state's history had scarred a half million acres and destroyed 350 homes and businesses a year earlier when seasonal rains were late. By mid-April of this year, a severe drought had dragged on for four months—and more than 2,000 fires had scorched some 50,000 acres, three times the loss by the same date the previous spring. National Guard helicopters scooped lake water into 750-gallon water bags to help quench a 2,400-acre fire on the eastern coast, twin fires that charred 3,800 acres farther south and a mile-wide wall of flames near the Lakeland airport at the center of the state (left). All told, 300,000 acres and 150 houses burned before the longed-for rains came in June—serious losses, to be sure, but less dire than many had feared.

Apr. 5 Libya delivers two suspects in the 1988 **Pan Am Flight 103** bombing—which killed 270 people over Lockerbie, Scotland—to the Netherlands for a trial under Scottish law.

Apr. 5 A 21-year-old roofer pleads guilty in Colorado to the 1998 **kidnapping and murder** of Matthew Shepard, a gay college student. Russell Henderson, the first of two men to stand trial for the crime, is sentenced to two consecutive life terms.

Apr. 9 Niger's President Ibrahim Bare Mainassara, who seized power in a 1996 coup, **is himself assassinated** in a military takeover.

Apr. 11 Putter nonpareil José María Olazábal, 33, wins the 63rd **Masters Tournament** at the Augusta National Golf Club in Georgia. It is the Spaniard's second Masters win.

Sweet Relief

When the Serbs' horrific ethnic cleansing campaign drove them from their homeland, more than 400,000 Kosovars flooded into Kukes, 15 miles across the Albanian border. Though the town's camps were overcrowded and perilously close to Serbian shelling, many refugees refused efforts to move them farther south. Here, they hoped to find lost relations crossing into the country. Jubilant reunions occurred often, including this one among members of two-year-old Agim Shala's large, close-knit clan, who had watched daily for the baby's grandparents. When relatives spotted them outside a camp fence, they passed Agim through for a long-delayed hug. Within Kosovar families, "separation is an almost unheard-of concept," says one refugee advocate. "People could not stand to be apart."

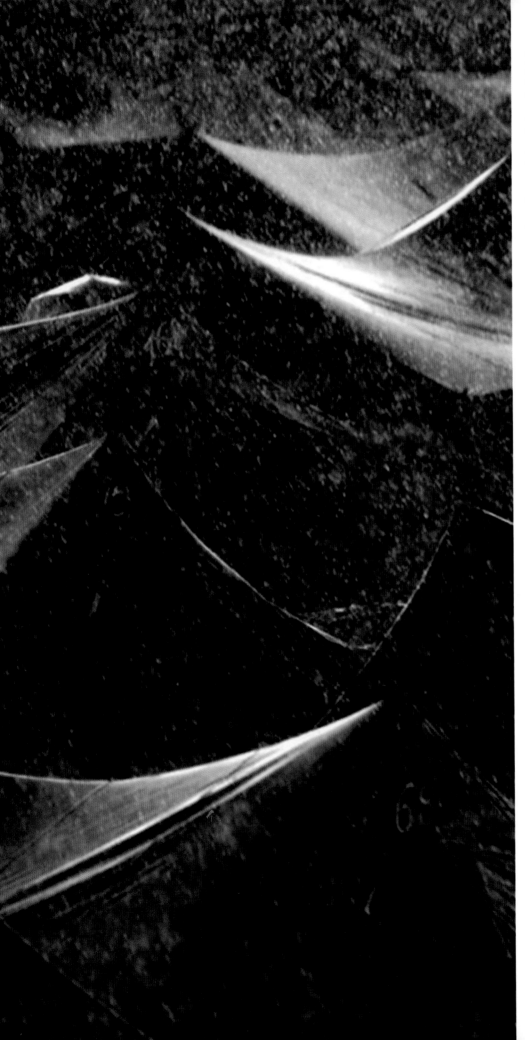

Apr. 16 After DNA tests, Donna Fasano, who gave birth to black and white fraternal twin boys in December because of an **embryo mix-up** at a Manhattan fertility clinic, agrees to give the black baby to Deborah Rogers, an African American whose fertilized egg was mistakenly implanted in Fasano.

Apr. 20 Gov. Christine Whitman concedes that some New Jersey state troopers **practice racial profiling**, routinely stopping black and Hispanic motorists in misguided attempts to crack down on drug trafficking. The American Civil Liberties Union will soon release its own findings: Officers across the U.S. systematically engage in the practice.

Apr. 23 In the shadow of month-old air strikes against Yugoslavia, NATO marks its **50th anniversary** with a somber summit meeting in Washington, D.C.

Apr. 23 Paleontologists report that 2.5-million-year-old bones and a skull found in Ethiopia may represent distant, but direct, **human ancestors**— who first branched off from apes about five million years ago.

Wartime Way Stations

The refugees kept coming, wave after weary wave. As war ravaged Kosovo, Macedonia grudgingly accepted some 100,000 ethnic Albanians; the poorest country in Europe, Albania welcomed more than 450,000. To shelter the diaspora, dozens of tent cities—from villages of 2,000 (like this one in Tirana, Albania's capital) to settlements of tens of thousands— were thrown together. In most camps conditions were grim, but many of the dispossessed soon found more substantial shelter: Thousands of Albanians opened their homes, eventually taking in most of the refugees.

Apr. 25 Taking authorities by surprise, more than **10,000 peaceful protesters** quietly assemble outside China's leadership compound seeking recognition of their sect, Falun Gong. The government will later ban the 100-million-member group, saying it threatens social stability.

May 1 Following a personal appeal by Rev. Jesse Jackson, Yugoslav President Slobodan Milosevic agrees to the release of three **U.S. soldiers captured** more than a month earlier near the Serbia-Macedonia border.

May 2 On the floor of the Atlantic 300 miles off the Florida coast, salvagers locate Gus Grissom's *Mercury* **space capsule,** which filled with water and sank after Grissom had been safely picked up nearly 38 years ago. Two months later, the capsule will be recovered.

Whaling Rights

The Makah tribe's early-morning whale hunt off remote Neah Bay in Washington was traditional and . . . not. As local television viewers watched live, Makah hunters used harpoons and .50-caliber bullets to kill a 30-foot female. The tribe had not hunted whales for at least 70 years, ever since commercial whaling nearly wiped out the creatures. But the population has recovered and the California gray whale was removed from the endangered species list in 1994, allowing the Makah to harvest a few each year. Protesters fear the return of widespread whaling, but the Makah have agreed not to sell their catch. After the May hunt, members rendered blubber into oil, portioned meat out to families and feasted—some with more gusto than others—on the rest.

May 1 An American expedition finds the body of British mountaineer George Mallory 75 years **after his disappearance** just short of the 29,028-foot peak of Mount Everest. Mallory died almost three decades before the first recognized successful ascent.

May 6 AT&T positions itself to become the nation's **largest cable operator** by agreeing to acquire MediaOne (for some $58 billion). After FCC approval, AT&T will be able to deliver telephone services, interactive television and high-speed Internet access.

May 7 A Michigan jury orders *The Jenny Jones Show* to **pay $25 million** to the family of Scott Amedure, who was killed by Jonathan Schmitz, another male guest, after taping an episode that never aired. During the taping, Amedure revealed that he had a crush on Schmitz. The show's parent company will appeal, citing a "profoundly chilling effect" on other talk shows.

Monster Maelstrom

Heading home after seeing her husband off at Oklahoma City's airport, Tammy Holmgren heard tornado warnings on her van's radio. Soon she was driving through lashing winds, rain and hail. She pulled into an underpass, where photographer J. Pat Carter had also sought shelter. Carter fought the gale to open the van doors, pull out Tammy's two daughters and help tuck them against support pillars. The twister, one of 74 generated by a huge storm system over a five-state area, roared by the underpass, then spun (left) toward Oklahoma City's suburbs, where it blasted apart some 1,780 homes and took 36 lives. The mile-wide juggernaut had the highest winds ever recorded: 318 mph. Incredibly, the Holmgrens and Carter were unhurt—though her girls, says Tammy, still crawl into her bed at night whenever they hear the wind rise.

Slight Resemblance

By Windsor standards, the June wedding of publicist Sophie Rhys-Jones and Prince Edward, the queen's youngest child, was almost funky. The couple picked the chapel at Windsor over the formidable churches where Edward's siblings began their luckless adventures in matrimony. Sophie and her father were ferried in the queen's Rolls-Royce, but Edward came on foot. Only 560 guests attended, and ladies were asked not to wear hats (the 98-year-old Queen Mum wore one anyway; she can do anything she likes). As Rhys-Jones walked down the aisle in a shimmery beaded gown, Edward gave her a broad grin—and a playful, unprincelike wink. It bodes well.

May 7 On a NATO mission, a U.S. B-2 stealth bomber destroys Belgrade's Chinese Embassy, killing three and wounding more than 20. NATO and U.S. officials call the incident a **"tragic mistake,"** conceding that they had been misled by outdated maps.

May 8 The 157-year-old Citadel graduates its first female cadet, Nancy Mace, 21. The South Carolina military school began admitting women in 1996 after the Supreme Court struck down **an all-male policy** at Virginia Military Institute—which graduates two women this month.

May 15 Days after firing his third prime minister in 14 months, President **Boris Yeltsin narrowly survives** impeachment votes in the Duma, the lower chamber of Russia's parliament.

May 17 Ehud Barak, **a former general,** unseats Israel's incumbent prime minister, Benjamin Netanyahu.

Runaway Plane

As American Airlines Flight 1420 approached Little Rock National Airport just before midnight on June 1, weather conditions were an ominous brew: a raging thunderstorm, driving rain, hail, gusting winds. The plane touched down but then careened along the rain-slicked landing strip. It was still moving at 90 mph when it lurched beyond the runway and hurtled down an embankment, where it smashed into steel landing-light stanchions. Torn apart, the fuselage caught fire as passengers escaped. All but 11 of the 145 aboard survived; victims included Richard Buschmann, the 48-year-old pilot. Investigators are looking into why wing flaps never opened, and are also asking a more troubling question: Given the weather, why did a seasoned pilot decide to land at all?

Rallying Cries

Bloody uprisings in 1998 had at last put an end to President Suharto's decades-long stranglehold on Indonesia. In June of '99, voters took to the streets campaigning for their candidates in the first free general elections in 44 years. Suharto's party lost, paving the way for a new president in October: the physically frail Abdurrahman Wahid, a respected Muslim leader and scholar. He inherits a country hobbled by corruption, ethnic conflict and, most recently, a ghastly killing spree by pro-Jakarta militias following East Timor's vote for independence.

May 20 Thomas Solomon, a 15-year-old student at a Georgia high school, **wounds six students** with a .22-caliber rifle just one month after 15 died in the Columbine High shootings.

May 20 Robbie Knievel, 37, son of daredevil Evel Knievel, completes a 228-foot **motorcycle leap** over the Grand Canyon—a feat that the National Park Service had prevented his father from attempting 25 years earlier.

May 25 In a case that challenges the notorious "blue wall of silence," New York City police officer Justin Volpe **pleads guilty**—after coworkers give incriminating testimony—to four federal charges stemming from the 1997 torture and sodomizing of a Haitian immigrant.

June 5 German powerhouse Steffi Graf defeats top-seeded Martina Hingis to win **her sixth French Open;** one day later, American Andre Agassi will prevail over Ukraine's Andrei Medvedev to capture his first French Open.

A Fragile Peace

Yugoslav commanders and NATO representatives sparred for five grueling days at a French air base in Macedonia before announcing an end to the 11-week war in Kosovo (at right, Serbs sit at the far side of the table; NATO's Kosovo commander, Sir Mike Jackson, is at the head). The pact called for an immediate cease-fire and a gradual withdrawal of Serbian troops. Days after the signing, reports that the Kosovo Liberation Army (the ethnic Albanians' rebel force) had engaged in grisly reprisals against hundreds of Serbs made reining in the KLA a priority. "Sometimes," said U.N. Ambassador Richard Holbrooke, who went to Kosovo in late summer, "forging a peace is more difficult than winning a war."

June 5 Dark horse Lemon Drop Kid, at 29–1 odds, wins horse racing's **Belmont Stakes,** upsetting the Triple Crown hopes of Charismatic (who breaks a leg during the race and will be put out to stud).

June 12 Three days after Yugoslavia signs a cease-fire agreement with NATO, some 200 Russian troops **commandeer the Pristina airport,** a move that threatens to undermine peacekeeping efforts in war-ravaged Kosovo. The face-off is resolved six days later.

June 16 Acting on a tip from a viewer of *America's Most Wanted,* the FBI apprehends accused terrorist bomber Kathleen Ann Soliah, a former member of the **Symbionese Liberation Army.** Other members of the group achieved notoriety for their 1974 kidnapping of 19-year-old newspaper heiress Patty Hearst.

Hero's Welcome

Frail but spirited, Pope John Paul II was welcomed ebulliently at each stop on his high-speed, 21-city Polish tour. In the city of Sosnowiec (left), in a sorely depressed mining region, 320,000 believers gathered for an outdoor Mass. As they had hoped, the 79-year-old pontiff spoke out against capitalism's "dangers" and the "misery and suffering of those who cannot find their place." In Warsaw, even former communists stood and applauded when Solidarity's spiritual leader arrived in Parliament. He prayed with Jewish leaders and beatified 108 Roman Catholics killed by Nazis. Though a fever kept him from a major open-air Mass in Kraków, the pope managed a sentimental stop in his hometown before flying to Rome. "Long live the pope!" shouted the citizens of Wadowice. "You are right," he said with a smile. "I am still alive."

June 16 Thabo Mbeki is inaugurated as South Africa's second **postapartheid president,** succeeding Nelson Mandela.

June 21 Joseph Hazelwood, captain of the *Exxon Valdez,* which ran aground in 1989 and dumped 11 million gallons of crude oil, begins 1,000 hours of community service—**by picking up trash** in Anchorage, Alaska. Hazelwood was convicted, despite lengthy legal appeals, of "negligent discharge of oil."

June 30 Ending independent counsel Kenneth Starr's **five-year investigation** of the Clintons' Arkansas business dealings, Webster Hubbell, Hillary Clinton's former law partner, agrees to plead guilty to making false statements and evading income taxes. The judge fines Hubbell $125 and, on Starr's recommendation, adds no jail time.

Ease On Down

How do you move a lighthouse? Very, very slowly. When the Cape Hatteras Lighthouse was built in 1870, it stood almost a quarter mile back from the Outer Banks' harsh surf. But relentless erosion along the North Carolina coastline left the landmark a perilous 120 feet from the sea. In June the National Park Service began a $12 million, 2,900-foot move inland. Propelled by hydraulic jacks on steel tracks slicked with soap, the 4,830-ton tower traveled a stately foot per minute, arriving at its site 23 days later—a week ahead of schedule. Some 4,000 onlookers cheered as the structure came to a stop. "This move is part of our heritage," said one. The nation's tallest lighthouse should reopen for visitors by Memorial Day, 2000.

"You had the audacity to go on national TV, show the world what you did and dare the prosecution to stop you. Well, sir, consider yourself stopped."

Judge Jessica Cooper, sentencing Dr. Jack Kevorkian to prison for second-degree murder

Quiet, please

Trailblazing Brooklyn, Ohio, Mayor John Coyne pushed for the first seatbelt law 33 years ago. In '99, his town was the first to limit driving while talking on a cell phone. Coyne was unseated in the November elections. Phone-in votes?

The Backstreet Boys

In '99, no one else comes close to the larger-than-life success of *Millennium:* one week, 1.1 million albums sold.

THE POWER OF PINK

After 19 nominations, good sport Susan Lucci finally won an Emmy. The soap star promises to give it a good home.

Musical easels

Cézanne's *Still Life with Curtain, Pitcher and Bowl of Fruit* set a record for the Postimpressionist's work, selling at Sotheby's for $60.5 million to an anonymous telephone bidder. Mysteriously resold, the oil later surfaced at the Bellagio Hotel in Las Vegas.

Child, found

Incas sacrificed this young girl and two other children some 500 years ago. Their remains were discovered this year, so well preserved in Argentina's chill mountain air that scientists expect to learn a great deal from them.

"I had to set my priorities straight."

Vance Rego, who quit his job so he could line up early for tickets to *The Phantom Menace*

Jarring?

George Lucas's *Phantom Menace*, the *Star Wars* prequel, broke a box office record by taking in $28.5 million its first day, but character **Jar Jar Binks's** West Indian–ish accent generated a little controversy. One Web site: diediediejarjar.com.

"I'd like to name the baby America."

Naim Karaliju, a Kosovar refugee whose wife gave birth to a son just after arriving at Fort Dix, N.J.

"Kosovo is now one of the largest crime scenes in history."

Louis Freeh, FBI director, explaining why FBI agents had been sent to the Yugoslav province

"Now, say television was there on the beach on D-Day. What would we report? Equipment broke down, soldiers were confused, some died by friendly fire, some couldn't reach their objective … We would want investigations, we would want inquiries, we would recall General Eisenhower."

Filmmaker Barry Levinson, in a commencement address at American University

> "Women pay for contraceptives, and insurance companies pay for Viagra. What's wrong with this picture?"

Rep. James C. Greenwood (R-Pa.), introducing legislation to include contraceptives in health coverage

TURN OF TWO CENTURIES

	1899	1999
Percentage of the population in **RURAL AREAS**	60	25
Percentage of the population in **URBAN AREAS**	40	75
Percentage of the workforce employed in **AGRICULTURE**	39.6	2.5

A royal pain
The exquisite monarch butterfly, whose winter migration can cover up to 2,200 miles, is endangered—vulnerable to a multitude of threats. Genetically altered corn pollen appears to be one of them, but research this year was not conclusive.

And Elvis?
The Post Office invites you to vote on subjects of stamps to celebrate the '90s, but earlier decades are already settled. New in May: this salute to the "I Like Ike" era.

Promise not to tell?
The reclusive J.D. Salinger saw his love letters to writer Joyce Maynard sell for $156,000 (to a purchaser who returned them to Salinger). Now J.D.'s daughter is writing a memoir.

Starry, starry nights
Janet Leigh wore this Edith Head creation at the 1959 Academy Awards. This year it fetched $30,000 as one of 54 Oscar-going gowns auctioned to benefit AIDS research.

It's outta here!
Some venerable baseball venues are retiring in 2000:
TIGER STADIUM; Detroit, opened in 1912
CANDLESTICK/3COM PARK; San Francisco, 1960
ASTRODOME; Houston, 1965
KINGDOME; Seattle, 1976

> That "Love Thy Neighbor" thing...
> I meant that.
>
> —God

You might want to pay attention

Cattle Call

Chicago is such a cowish place, so rich in cow lore. Mrs. O'Leary's pesky cow, or at least the legend of same. Those famous, if unlovely, stockyards of yore. Cowtown. The illustrious NBA team (all right, it's named for boy cows). What better spot to mount an alfresco art exhibit of 301 charming bovines? Inspired on a trip abroad by a citywide "Cow Parade" in Zurich, a Chicago shoe store owner persuaded local businesses and cultural institutions to sponsor (each cow cost $2,000 to $3,000 to host) this show. Fiberglass figures were handed over to Chicago artists, who applied everything from zebra stripes (*Incowgnito*) to postage stamps (*Stampede*, natch). The whole herd was put out to pasture all over Chicowgo from June through October. Children scrambled over them, tourists took endless pictures (and left some $100 million in revenue). After the cows were carted away, 140 of them were auctioned for charity—Oprah herself bought three—raising almost $3.5 million. Moovelous.

"I never thought I'd say this about a cow, but they're enchanting."

Lois Weisberg, Chicago's commissioner of cultural affairs

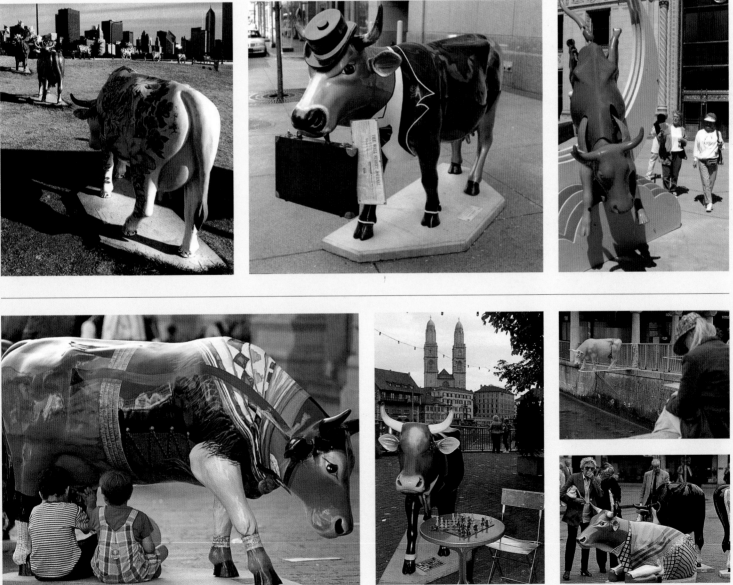

TOP ROW, LEFT TO RIGHT: RICH SAAL/THE STATE JOURNAL-REGISTER; JIM FROST/CHICAGO SUN TIMES; JEFF HAYNES/AFP. BOTTOM ROW: CAROLINE MINJOLLE/LOOKAT PHOTOS (4)

Opposite: A gilded cow strikes a pose on a Michigan Avenue meridian. Above, clockwise from top left: promenading cows; a business cow; a moon-jumper in front of the Wrigley Building; last year, in Zurich, cows prepared to take a dive, lolled in a city square, played chess and got "milked." New York City plans to round up a herd of more than 500 all-new cows for its own exhibit in the summer of 2000.

Superstars

In the U.S. soccer team's World Cup semifinal win over Brazil, Mia Hamm went high for a header. In a Houston win over the Charlotte Sting, Cynthia Cooper soared above Dawn Staley for an easy layup. Posters of Hamm and Cooper adorn the bedroom walls of thousands of little girls in the new age of women's sports.

You Go, Girls!

Only yesterday, most sports in America could be easily classified by gender, and to traipse onto the other fellow's—or gal's—field was to risk being seen as unfeminine or unmasculine, a tomboy or a girly-man. Football and ice hockey were, certifiably, Boys' Sports; softball and field hockey were Girls' Sports. Basketball was Boys', half-court basketball was Girls'. Baseball: Boys'. Cheerleading: Girls'. Soccer was neither. Soccer was Theirs, as in Europe's, as in Brazil's, as in Not Ours.

Time changes everything but not always of its own volition. About 30 years ago some clear-eyed folk realized that a nation boasting Equality as a trademark was, at the same time, fostering some serious inequities in the workplace, in the classroom and, yes, on the playground. Congress saw wisdom in the argument, and in 1972 passed its landmark Title IX legislation.

Barriers Fall

Jenny Thompson (left) broke records in the individual medley and the freestyle at a meet in Australia. In Germany, U.S. Open champ Serena Williams (below, at the Open) beat sister Venus for the first time in a tournament final. Soccer player Brandi Chastain (opposite, top) and teammate Briana Scurry helped set new ratings and attendance standards for women's sports.

"We are doing it, and we are right in your face."

U.S. World Cup soccer player Kristine Lilly

Title IX mandated, among other things, equal opportunity and spending for Girls' Sports, which could be Any and All Sports. In the ensuing years, even such high-minded institutions as Brown University were sued for giving boys a better shake. Courts sided with the girls, and schools got the message. Pioneers started lacing up hockey skates, donning Little League caps and even strapping on shoulder pads. Quickly, pioneers gave way to the next generation—a swarm of girls who fully expected to be allowed to play. Those girls have grown, and they've grown into winners.

This story began to unfold at the 1996 Atlanta Olympics when the U.S. women's basketball and soccer teams were among the most spectacular athletes in town. At Nagano, two years later, a bunch of U.S. professional hockey players—men—disgraced themselves by losing early, getting mad and trashing their Olympic Village rooms. As the guys were tossing chairs around, a bunch of U.S. amateur hockey players—women—captured the public's heart and won the first-ever Olympic gold medal in their sport. These stories, and the individual glories achieved by others such as track star Gail Devers (Olympic gold, 1992 and '96), swimmer Jenny Thompson (five Olympic golds, 1992 and '96) and skier Picabo Street (Olympic silver, 1994, and gold, '98), can now be seen as prelude to the events of 1999. In the last year of the millennium, the American Woman Athlete took on the world, twisted the world's arm behind its back and made the world cry uncle.

U.S. women since Helen Wills in the Roaring '20s have been good at tennis, but women's tennis has never seen anything like the roaring Williams sisters of Compton, Calif. Big, bold bashers of the ball, they, along with their even taller countrywoman Lindsay Davenport, have rewritten the rules of their sport. When Switzerland's Martina Hingis came to the fore a couple of years ago with her Chris Evert smile and her Chris Evert style of play, it looked like she might be in for a long run at the top. Ha! Davenport dismantled Hingis in the 1998 U.S. Open finals; this year Serena Williams dismissed her in straight sets to become the first African American woman to win the U.S. title since Althea Gibson in 1958. Serena, then 17, is five foot eleven and 145 pounds; her sister Venus, 19, is six foot one and 165 pounds; Davenport, 23, is six foot two and 155 pounds. Venus hit a serve at Wimbledon last year that was clocked at 125 mph; after winning the Open, Serena suggested she might try the men's draw in 2000. They won't let her, of course, and it's probably a good thing for the boys.

The Williams sisters hit hard; Madame Butterfly hits harder.

HECTOR MATA/AFP

CHRIS TROTMAN/DUOMO

JEAN CATUFFE/SIPA PRESS

"It has taken 25 years to make a champion. You're seeing the first blush of what happens when you give women the chance to play."

Donna Lopiano, executive director of the Women's Sports Foundation

Stealing Thunder

At the World Championships in Seville, the exploits of Marion Jones (above) overshadowed her husband's win in the shot put. In a game against defending Little League world champs Toms River, N.J., Vickie Waterman (left) stole the spotlight from the boys. In her win over April Fowler, even Laila Ali's triumphant pose (opposite) recalled her old man.

She is Laila Ali, Muhammad Ali's 21-year-old daughter and a woman touted as the Great Black Hope of women's boxing, a game heretofore dominated by Floridian Christy Martin. In a year that saw a woman beat up a man (Margaret McGregor decisioned Loi Chow), Ali made like her dad and, with charisma and a lopsided win, elevated her sport. The five-foot-ten, 168-pound Ali won her supermiddleweight debut with a 31-second knockout of April Fowler, a waitress who, as a boxer, is a superb waitress. Even if Ali has been seen only briefly, she clearly has the goods. "Laila looked like Muhammad when she boxed," said her mother, sitting ringside in the sellout crowd of 2,600 at an upstate New York casino. "She looked like a boxer, not a woman."

Cynthia Cooper looks like a woman and a basketball star. She is a five-foot-ten, 150-pound shooting guard for the WNBA champion Houston Comets who fought through an extremely tough season to bring her team its third straight championship. Women's pro hoops has no shortage of marquee talent these days, especially with the supremely talented Chamique Holdsclaw now in the fold, but Cooper still rules. She is the Michael Jordan of women's roundball, possessing all of MJ's style, leadership ability and stoicism in the clutch. Cooper's mother died of breast cancer last year and her friend and teammate, Kim Perrot, lost her battle with lung cancer, yet Cooper led the league in scoring for a third straight year, then won her third straight championship-series MVP trophy. "We had to win it with broken hearts," Cooper said as she wore Perrot's jersey in the locker room. "I think Kim is proud." Of Cooper, Perrot certainly would be. At 36, having fought her way out of Watts to find surprising opportunities for women in sports, Cooper is one of an older generation who was able to take advantage—and continues to. Jenny Thompson, soon to turn 27 (ancient by swimming standards), is still setting world records and is intending to compete in the 2000 Summer Olympics in Sydney, Australia. That's another thing the rise of the woman athlete in America has afforded: the chance to compete longer, while actually making a living at the game.

Much of the U.S. women's soccer team has been together for the better part of a decade. In that time they have won World and Olympic titles and generally established themselves, along with teams from Brazil and China, as the planet's elite. But no earlier success prepared them for what happened when the U.S. hosted the 1999 World Cup tournament. On June 19 for the Americans' opener against Denmark, 80,000 fans packed Giants Stadium—setting a record for attendance at a women's sporting event. Three of the six U.S. matches—all of them wins—were sellouts. When Brandi Chastain finished the tournament with her winning penalty kick against China in Pasadena's packed Rose Bowl, 40 million were watching on TV, more than watched the finals of the NBA—

the *men's* NBA. The women's soccer team was accorded a transcendent, peculiarly American kind of fame, a celebrity fame that put them on the cover of *Time* and on the Letterman show, and that made them the only topic of conversation at the country's water coolers. No one could ignore these women.

Nor could sports fans ignore Marion Jones, who at 23 won gold (100 meters) and bronze (long jump) at the 1999 World Championships in Spain. Jones hopes to march at the 2000 Olympics beside Thompson and soccer stars Mia Hamm and Julie Foudy. Angelle Seeling of Luling, La., won't be there, but that's only because motorcycle racing isn't an Olympic sport. She won five races in the Winston Drag Racing Pro Stock Motorcycle series in '99, more than any of the guys. Vickie Waterman of Middleboro, Mass., won't be there either, but that's only because women's baseball isn't yet an Olympic sport and, besides, Vickie's only 12. In the New England Regional championships leading up to the Little League World Series, Vickie, a catcher, went 1 for 2 and scored a run. "I've never seen anyone knock her over," Ray Waterman said of his five-foot-three, 95-pound daughter. "But I have seen a lot of boys getting their wind knocked out of them trying to run into her."

In the new millennium, girls are knocking the wind out of boys. There's a lesson here, of course, and it's not just that girls are athletic or that girls like sports. The lesson is that anyone, given half a chance, might rise. Without Title IX, Mia Hamm might never have found her way to the soccer pitch, or Cynthia Cooper her way to the hoop. Yes, sure—not all of the women celebrated above went to college or played their sport even in high school. Madame Butterfly wasn't fighting unless in the schoolyard, and Angelle Seeling wasn't breaking speed limits unless on the highway. Moreover, Title IX has not righted all wrongs: While 2.6 million girls play high school or college sport, nearly a tenfold increase since 1972, the 2.6 million still represent only 40 percent of all scholastic or collegiate athletes. Nevertheless, the law has, over time, changed perception, and perception has changed reality. Today's girl says with confidence, "It's my turn at bat."

Behold the Boom

Most of us know the thunderlike crack of a plane breaking the sound barrier. Here is what that sound looks like—at least on a humid day. Shooting from an aircraft carrier off the coast of Japan, a Navy photographer caught a Hornet fighter going supersonic. Shock waves force a momentary condensation of water vapor (the cloud seen here). The same waves also send out that sonic boom, but in the fraction of a second it takes for the sound to reach the earth, the cloud has vanished.

Summer

July 7 President Clinton limits Brazilian steel imports and Australian and New Zealand lamb imports in an effort to preserve U.S. producers' profit margins and **prevent "dumping"** (sale of foreign products in the U.S. at below-market prices).

July 7 Having already paid more than $117 million to Jeffrey Katzenberg, the Walt Disney Company agrees to settle a **three-year dispute** with its former studio chief. The undisclosed terms are likely to cost Disney another $130 million.

July 7 A Florida jury holds that five tobacco companies misled consumers about cigarettes' health hazards and **may be held liable** for smokers' illnesses. It is the first class-action ruling against the tobacco industry.

July 8 University students in Tehran, protesting the government's shutdown of a moderate newspaper, are attacked by **Islamic vigilantes** and police, sparking six days of violent clashes.

Talk to Me

If you want to run for the U.S. Senate in a state where you've never resided, modesty isn't a bad approach. Hillary Clinton kicked off her unofficial campaign for the Senate with a three-day "listening tour" across central New York, inviting audiences to share their concerns. Between note-taking and sympathetic nods, the First Lady spoke about healthcare, education and creating jobs. One likely opponent, New York City Mayor Rudy Giuliani, also got a word in edgewise, declaring tongue-in-cheek that he just might run for senator—in Arkansas.

Aria Ahoy

Every summer, spectacular "floating" productions lure thousands to the opera festival in Bregenz, a lakeside Austrian resort. In 1999, Verdi's *A Masked Ball,* about the assassination of Swedish King Gustav III, made an unprecedented splash. Singers performed under the baleful gaze of an eight-story steel-and-fiberglass skeleton but at least didn't have to struggle to keep their balance: The stage—a giant "book of life"—was held fast by 200 pylons. At evening's end, the skeleton's left hand swept Gustav onto a coffin-barge, sending the unlucky king off into the night. The production will run again this year, but hurry: The ticket supply is sure to dry up.

July 12 Coca-Cola reports a drop in second-quarter earnings. The world's leading soft-drink maker had recalled **17 million cases** of soda—at a cost of $103 million—after hundreds of European consumers had complained of nausea, dizziness and headaches.

July 13 After a three-and-a-half-week nationwide manhunt, **"Railroad Killer"** Rafael Resendez-Ramirez—a suspect in the murders of eight people in three states—surrenders to Texas authorities.

July 24 Cary Stayner, a 37-year-old motel handyman, confesses to **beheading a woman** near her Yosemite home and to the earlier murders of three other women. The slayings had stymied federal investigators for months.

Not Groovy

The kids at the original Woodstock were packed in like sardines, but mellowness prevailed. Thirty years later, the throngs at Woodstock '99 ditched peace and harmony. After the last set, hundreds of shouting fans fed huge bonfires, burned vendors' trucks and tore down a metal equipment tower. Some blamed high prices—a bottle of water cost four dollars—some the brutal heat and charmless setting (a concrete-paved former Air Force base in Rome, N.Y.). But craziness was in the air from the beginning: Five women reported being raped, and the audience at one performance blindly threw rocks and bottles. This was no lovefest.

July 27 A flash flood sweeps away 21 **outdoor adventurers** in the Saxetenbach Gorge near Interlaken, Switzerland.

July 29 Atlanta day trader Mark Barton, who had **lost $105,000** on stock transactions in seven weeks, kills his wife and two children, then fatally shoots nine brokerage firm employees and wounds 13.

July 29 A federal judge who had found President Clinton in **contempt of court** for giving "intentionally false" testimony about his relationship with a former White House intern fines him $90,000.

Aug. 1 A record-breaking heat wave sweeps across the midwestern, southern and eastern states. **Thirty die** in Chicago in one weekend; high temperatures eventually claim some 300 lives nationally.

Hard Rain

Widespread flooding is an annual event in Asia, where the monsoon season brings battering rains for weeks on end. This year, rising waters and mudslides killed some 950 and drove millions from their homes in China, Japan, North and South Korea and Southeast Asia. Typhoon Olga left Chanthaburi, a coastal province in Thailand, largely submerged; floodwaters formed five-foot-deep rivers and coursed through its capital. After five days of deluge, the waters began to recede. While grown-ups carried on as best they could, some kids made the best of the disaster.

Aug. 1 Taiwanese-born scientist Wen Ho Lee, the focus of a **three-year FBI probe,** denies giving nuclear-weapons secrets to China. Wen was dismissed in March from the Los Alamos National Laboratory.

Aug. 4 Surrounded by family— including grandson Prince Charles and great-grandsons William and Harry— the Queen Mother celebrates **her 99th birthday** at her London home.

Aug. 11 In a victory for religious conservatives, the Kansas Board of Education eliminates the **teaching of evolution** from its mandatory science curriculum.

Aug. 14 Texas Gov. George W. Bush, aiming to become the Republican **presidential candidate,** wins 31 percent of the vote in the Iowa straw poll.

Today, at Daycare

Out of work, living in a trailer with his parents, Buford O. Furrow Jr., 37, was restless. So the former mechanic drove his van from Washington State to Los Angeles, where he walked into a Jewish community center, riddled its lobby with machine-gun fire and fled. The bullets wounded a receptionist, a teenage counselor and three children; police arrived, then led dozens of children across the street. Meanwhile, Furrow fatally shot Joseph Ileto, a Filipino American mail carrier who was making his rounds. A day later, in Las Vegas, Furrow turned himself in, reportedly telling the FBI that he was concerned about the decline of the white race. But he hadn't meant to harm the children, he said. "The kids," he reportedly told investigators, "got in the way."

DAVID BOHRER
LOS ANGELES TIMES

Taken by Surprise

Radar warned of an imminent thunderstorm, but what struck Salt Lake City moments later was a full-blown twister—a rarity in Utah, which is buffered by the Rockies. In five minutes the tornado tore a three-mile path through the city's heart, leveling 34 homes. One man was killed and more than 100 people were injured, many by debris that swirled in the 120-mph gusts. "It looked," said one stunned observer, "like the city dump was in the sky."

10 MIN PARKING

Aug. 19 In Belgrade's largest anti-Milosevic demonstration since the end of NATO's 78-day bombing campaign, **tens of thousands** of protesters demand the Yugoslav president's removal.

Aug. 23 Chancellor Gerhard Schröder returns Germany's **government headquarters** to Berlin a decade after the collapse of the Wall.

Aug. 25 Austrian police arrest Gen. Momir Talic, **the Bosnian Serb Army's chief of staff,** in Vienna. The International War Crimes Tribunal charges Talic with widespread persecution of non-Serbs from Bosnia during the war in the mid-'90s.

Aug. 25 After denying for more than six years that its agents in Waco, Tex., used pyrotechnic tear gas during the 1993 showdown with Branch Davidians, **the FBI recants.** Some eighty men, women and children died in the conflagration.

Under Wraps

It could have been cooked up in Hollywood: A donkey plodding along in Egypt's Bahariya Oasis stumbles when one leg slips into a small hole. The rider peers inside—and beholds shining stacks of gilded mummies. Fearing looters, archaeologists keep the dazzling find secret for three years, then announce that they have excavated 105 mummies, most sumptuously decorated—only the tip of the 2,000-year-old graveyard, which may turn out to hold 10,000 interred remains in all.

Aug. 28 Three astronauts abandon the orbiting *Mir* and **return to earth.** The Russian government plans to jettison the world's longest-used space station next year. Any parts that don't burn up on reentry are expected to land in the Pacific Ocean.

Aug. 30 East Timor residents defy threats of violence from pro-Jakarta militias to vote on **the territory's future.** Five days later, they deliver a resounding verdict: Nearly 80 percent favor independence.

Sept. 1 Vincent Jenkins, 60, leaves a New York State prison where he has served 17 years for rape. Jenkins is the 67th convicted prisoner in North America **to be cleared** by DNA evidence since 1989, when the technology was first used for exoneration.

Night and Day
When the moon passed between the sun and the earth on August 11, the path of its shadow swept across Europe and the Middle East and ended at the Bay of Bengal—a route that allowed billions to watch the last total eclipse of the millennium. In Jordan a photographer who lacked equipment to view the eclipse directly asked a stranger to hold out his hand—and captured the celestial show in the man's palm.

Sept. 1 Umpires' ill-fated negotiating tactic (more than 50 had **submitted resignations**) culminates in a settlement with Major League baseball: Twenty-two umps will collect their '99 pay and bonuses but lose their jobs.

Sept. 2 Scientists report that injecting mice with a modified gene **improves memory** and learning skills, raising the possibility that human cognition may also be enhanced one day.

Sept. 4 "You got me," says financier Martin Frankel to FBI agents who had tracked him through Europe for four months prior to his **capture in Hamburg,** Germany. Frankel will be indicted on 36 federal counts for siphoning in excess of $200 million from insurance companies in five states.

Sept. 5 Israeli Prime Minister Ehud Barak signs an agreement to release 350 **political prisoners** and transfer 18 percent of the West Bank to Palestinian authorities in exchange for a crackdown on terrorism.

Labor of Loss

Two days after northwest Turkey's massive earthquake, weak cries still came from the ruins of the shoddily built high-rises that had collapsed like cardboard. Forty thousand may have perished in the disaster. Some of those trapped alive in the debris were pulled to safety, but chaotic rescue efforts left many others to suffer slow deaths. Victims were buried in mass graves, including this one at the quake's epicenter, 55 miles east of Istanbul. Though the temblor was unusually severe—7.4 on the Richter scale— its grievous toll cannot be blamed on nature alone.

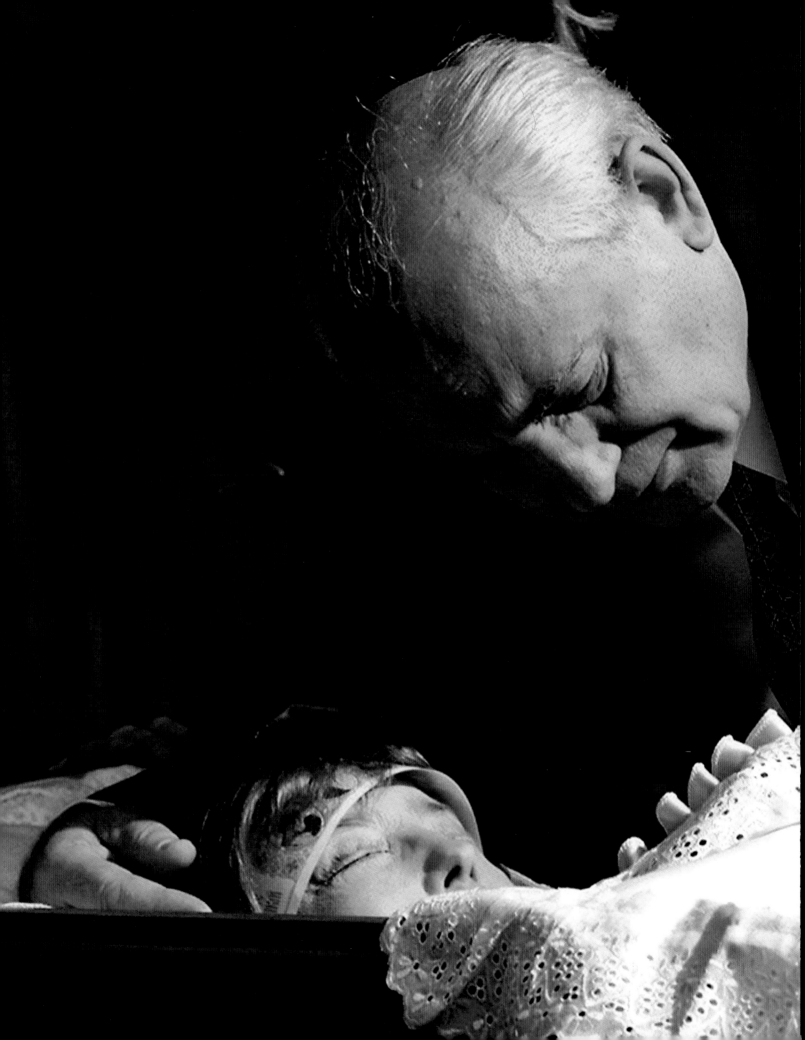

Sept. 7 In the largest media merger ever, Viacom announces plans to acquire CBS for $35 billion. If approved, the deal will create the world's **second-largest media company** (after Time Warner).

Sept. 7 A magnitude 5.8 earthquake in Greece rips through Athens, **killing 143** and injuring some 1,600.

Sept. 10 Over many objections, President Clinton frees 11 members of a militant Puerto Rican nationalist group. Convicted of committing numerous **terrorist acts** in the '70s and '80s, they vow to renounce violence in exchange for their release.

Sept. 11 Serena Williams, 17, defeats Martina Hingis to win the United States Open **women's singles.** The next day, she and her sister Venus will capture the women's doubles title, while Andre Agassi will defeat Todd Martin in the men's singles final.

Loving Farewell

Russians didn't know what to make of her. Rejecting the invisibility expected of Kremlin wives, she traveled abroad, spoke her mind in public (Sen. Barbara Mikulski called her the only person "who talks more than I do") and flashed her radiant smile at reporters. Nancy Reagan didn't warm to her—the opinionated ex-sociology professor and the iron-willed former MGM starlet were both too alike and too different. But Raisa's husband adored her. Former Soviet President Mikhail Gorbachev bent over his wife's open casket, after her death from leukemia at 67, and tenderly stroked her face and hair.

Sept. 15 Unemployed day laborer Larry Ashbrook, 47, **opens fire** during a Baptist church service in Fort Worth, killing seven and injuring seven more before fatally turning the gun on himself.

Sept. 16 Microsoft chairman Bill Gates and his wife, Melinda, create a $1 billion college scholarship fund (the largest such gift ever) to **encourage minority presence** in colleges and in the fields of math and science.

Sept. 20 U.N.-backed peacekeeping forces arrive in **East Timor** to contain the pro-Jakarta, militia-led violence that has swept the territory ever since residents voted for independence three weeks earlier.

Sept. 30 In the worst nuclear accident in Japan's history, workers at a Tokaimura energy plant mix **dangerous levels of uranium** with nitric acid, setting off a runaway reaction that exposes 69 workers to high levels of radiation, critically injuring three.

Trashed

Coffins floated in its khaki-colored floodwaters; so did the foul overflow from sewage plants and hog-waste lagoons, pesticides from wiped-out warehouses, and about three million livestock carcasses. (At right, hogs struggle in rising waters.) Hurricane Floyd churned across a dozen states. In eastern North Carolina, it was catastrophic: 50 lives lost and an estimated $1.7 billion in damages. Development in the low-lying region, where wetlands have been farmed and floodplains paved, made the area especially vulnerable.

On Shaky Ground

When the earth's crust buckled, most of Taiwan's inhabitants were sleeping. The magnitude 7.6 quake struck on September 21 just before two a.m., entombing more than 2,300 in thousands of collapsed buildings. The hard-hit town of Chi-Chi, seen here, is 90 miles south of Taipei, the island's capital. But even after the initial quake, the ground did not stay still: Within the week, thousands of aftershocks struck, 11 of which qualified as serious earthquakes themselves.

Stop fidgeting!

Cuba's chief was inducted into Madame Tussaud's Wax Museum this summer, and the replica (above) sported boots and fatigues donated by El Presidente himself. Not shy, and certainly not retiring, Fidel Castro nevertheless showed a becoming modesty about the figure's debut. "It has been for me a great honor," he said, "much more than I deserve."

"Big Bird is nearly 30 years old, and it's time to leave the federal nest."

Representative Steve Largent (R-Okla.), on federal support for public TV

"I'm hopeful that this can be resolved in a constructive way so Big Bird can remain on the air."

Representative Tom Davis (R-Va.), on the same subject

THE POWER OF PINK

Entertainer of the Year Shania Twain impressed us much by kicking the Country Music Awards into high gear.

Does she or . . .

At opening ceremonies for golf's Ryder Cup, in Brookline, Mass., no one knew that the American team would stage a world-class come-from-behind victory, or that the team outfits (recycled, it appeared, from great-aunt Irma's slipcovers) would create a minor media tempest. But team members' wives and girlfriends (Tiger Woods's pal Joanna Jagoda is in front) got only high marks for their sartorial solidarity.

Wiz kid

Luckily for his legions of fans, Hogwarts School of Witchcraft and Wizardry's most famous pupil is adventure-prone. English author J.K. Rowling followed up her first Harry Potter book, a runaway hit, with two more volumes—both of which became best-sellers before their official debuts.

"We haven't had this much excitement . . . since Banjo Greenfield's son Dozer towed his double-wide through town."
Matt Major of Skaneateles, N.Y., on the Clintons vacationing in his town

"We like to knock people's heads off, and then put on a skirt and go dance."
Brandi Chastain, U.S. women's soccer team

RoboPup!

Technogeek man's best friend may become AIBO, the first robotic dog. Sony's high-performance-plastic, $2,500 pooch walks, waves a paw, barks and responds to touch, sound and visual cues. AIBO can't smell, but never mind—he has a camera up his nose anyway.

FLASHBACK: TURN OF TWO CENTURIES

	1899	1999
Percentage of high school graduates, compared with the population 17 years of age	6	69*
Average number of people per household	4.76	2.64

*Estimated

Hair-raisers

One was shot in a speedy eight days (and nights!) and starred unknowns; the other had a big-studio budget and a known, one Bruce Willis. But both summer chillers made their bones: Mockumentary *Blair Witch Project* hit $50 million in a week; *The Sixth Sense,* with 10-year-old Haley Joel Osment (above) and a whammy ending, became the 12th-biggest grosser ever.

Don't make me come down there.

—God

You might want to pay attention

Well, I declare

Among those considering a run for President:

Warren Beatty
Cybill Shepherd
Donald Trump
Pat Buchanan
Gary Bauer
Orrin Hatch
Lyndon LaRouche

Perfect timing

He had wanted it—obsessed about it—for nearly a decade. In Seville, Michael Johnson got it: the world record (43.18) in the 400 meters. Even without his trademark golden shoes, Johnson shaved more than a tenth of a second off Butch Reynolds's 11-year-old mark. Precious mettle indeed.

Sweet dreams

Sega's Dreamcast video game system broke sales records right away. It will be a short reign: An even cooler Sony system is debuting in 2000.

Broadway boogie-woogie

A tribute to Great White Way songwriters continues the multiyear U.S.P.S. celebration of American music legends (the series started with, yes, Elvis, in 1993) with great composer-lyricist teams and other Tin Pan Alley denizens.

"I am having my DNA fumigated."

Carrie Fisher, who was unhappy with her father Eddie Fisher's tell-all memoir

The party's over

Feds shut down Nevada's 31-year-old Mustang Ranch after its owners were convicted of racketeering. Closing the country's first and biggest legal brothel left some of the working girls (and, no doubt, patrons) teary. Said one: "It's sure been a wild ride."

"It is harder to get a prescription filled than to buy a handgun."

Reverend Don Harp, during a memorial service for victims of Atlanta's day-trader shootings

Great white gator

Albino alligators are easy for predators to spot, but this guy, one of 17 known such specimens in the United States, has found a safe haven in a Dade County, Fla., wildlife park. His new digs will include a private pool and plenty of shade to protect that pigment-free hide.

Each day of the 21-day race, it grew harder to believe: A young American was conquering the most grueling course in bike racing, the Tour de France. And that wasn't even his toughest opponent—he had already beaten testicular cancer that had spread to his abdomen, lungs and brain. Lance Armstrong showed us something: how to persevere, cheerfully, in the face of the impossible. It didn't end there. In October his wife, Kristin, gave birth to their son, Luke (Armstrong had stored sperm before undergoing chemotherapy). The proud dad's advice? "If you ever get a second chance in life for something, go all the way."

A LESSON IN LIVING

The Comeback Kid

Patrick Ireland in a 1998 school yearbook photo

For the first 17 years of his life, it seemed as if no obstacle—physical or intellectual—was insurmountable for Patrick Ireland. In high school he maintained a 4.0 average. He won awards for waterskiing, fired three-pointers and blocked shots for his YMCA basketball team. He threw baseballs right-handed and wrote, in small, neat capital letters, with his left hand. "Lots of things came easy to me," he recalls. But that was before the late morning of Tuesday, April 20, when seniors Eric Harris and Dylan Klebold opened fire—

The Boy in the Window

Ireland's escape after the shooting at Columbine High School was televised live. The then unknown student instantly became famous. At the time, his injuries had impaired his vision, but he can recall "feeling the warm breeze, hearing the helicopters and the SWAT team yelling for me to jump."

with sawed-off shotguns, a rifle and a semiautomatic pistol—on their teachers and classmates at Columbine High School in Littleton, Colo. Ireland, then a junior, was studying in the library with his friends Makai Hall, Dan Steepleton, Stephen Austin Eubanks and Corey DePooter. Forewarned by the shouts of a teacher, the students were hiding under tables when the gunmen came in, told the "jocks" to stand, then began firing. DePooter was killed. Hall, Eubanks and Steepleton were wounded; Hall was shot in the leg. As Ireland reached to put pressure on his friend's leg to stop the bleeding, his head rose above the table. Patrick Ireland was shot three times, twice in the head and once in the right foot.

> "I told myself, 'If I'm going to survive, I've gotta get out of here.' I tried to stand but couldn't."

Healing

Above: Recovery involved daily rehabilitation sessions, including treatment with physical therapist Brian Trzaskos. Opposite: Less than three weeks after the shooting, Ireland and his parents, John and Kathy, answered reporters' questions at Craig Hospital.

Ireland floated in and out of consciousness for several hours. When he finally came to, the other survivors had already escaped. Unbeknownst to him, Harris and Klebold had shot themselves and lay dead in the library.

"I wasn't sure where they were," Ireland recalls. "I told myself, 'If I'm going to survive, I've gotta get out of here.' There was some fear and some, like, worry and sadness, about not letting people down, not letting the gunmen win. I tried to stand but couldn't." Remembering that day, he says, "I strove to survive."

His right side paralyzed, Ireland pushed himself across the room on his back with his left leg. When he reached the wall beneath a window, he propped his back against it, then, using a chair for support, pushed himself up with his left leg on his second try. He gradually lifted himself through the window and into the arms of a SWAT team crouched below, atop an armored truck.

For the first week after the shooting, Ireland's mind was like a computer with damaged circuits. One bullet had passed through the left hemisphere of the brain, which controls language, complex thinking and the right side of the body. The bullet remains lodged in Ireland's head, too risky to remove; his brain is healing around it. As a result, Ireland talked to visitors in Spanish (he had recently returned from a class trip to Spain), quoted dialogue from movies and recited the capital cities of South America from memory (a week earlier, he had taken a test with geography questions).

"Even if people understood what I was saying, I might be saying something totally different from what I wanted to say."

On July 2, Ireland was released from Craig Hospital, the renowned brain and spinal injury rehabilitation center in Denver. That same day, an 11 a.m. press conference caused him to miss his therapy. He made it up in the afternoon, determined not to let anything interfere with his recovery.

GEORGE KOCHANIEC/ROCKY MOUNTAIN NEWS–CORBIS SYGMA

Back to School

Above: Ireland was well enough by Columbine High School's August 16 reopening to attend classes in the mornings. (He will graduate on time, in May 2000.) Right: On September 24, classmates crowned Ireland their Homecoming King. "He's always putting others before himself," said one.

His improvement has been as gradual and noticeable as the growth spurt that took Ireland (who turned 18 in the hospital) from five foot eleven in April to six foot two by autumn. Visiting with him near year's end, one sees that when he gestures to emphasize a point, it is with his left hand. The right hand is still partially paralyzed and stays in his lap. He walks with a slight list to starboard; his right leg is stabilized by a brace that runs from the ball of his foot to beneath his knee.

The A student of other semesters had to resume schoolwork with baby steps. His initial rehabilitation therapy included relearning how to recognize numbers and letters. "It was hard to write a word, then sentences, then paragraphs," says Ireland, who had to leave school early many days for afternoon therapy sessions. "It's been like doing 11 years of school in six months."

Progress was measured in other ways, too. In November, after vision exams and practice at a computer simulator and behind the wheel, Ireland made his first extended solo excursion since the shooting, driving 22 miles round-trip from his home to school to Craig Hospital. Like its owner, Ireland's car, a 1989 Ford Probe, is carrying temporary modifications. The gas pedal has been adjusted so he can control it with his left foot. A knob on the steering wheel allows for one-handed driving. A remote activates the Pearl Jam, Matchbox 20 and Shania Twain CDs in his dashboard player.

Instead of hiding from the consequences of his ordeal, Ireland chose to confront them—in carefully selected interviews and in his college application essay, an account of what happened in the library. With his refusal to yield to fear or his own body, then and since, Ireland became what history may regard as a late 20th century phenomenon: a personality so immediately famous for a single act that he's known by his headline rather than his name.

Among the letters that poured into Craig Hospital and Columbine High was mail addressed simply "The Boy in the Window, Littleton, Colorado." As with "Santa Claus, North Pole," there was no doubting who it was meant for.

Instead of hiding from the consequences of his ordeal, Ireland has chosen to confront them.

Swallowed by the Sea

"My baby, my baby," wailed one woman after the oceanside service in Newport, R.I., for the 217 who died when EgyptAir Flight 990 plunged into the chill waters off the New England coast. More than 250 relatives and friends attended the multifaith ceremony; afterward, many walked to the windswept water's edge to offer private goodbyes. Voice and data recorders failed to lay the mystery of the crash to rest: Why did an apparently problem-free plane plummet through the clear night sky? Investigators speculated—although Egyptians angrily protested—that a copilot in the Boeing 767 meant to commit suicide. The bereaved could only wait for answers, and mourn.

Fall

CORBIS SYGMA

Oct. 2 Testing part of a missile defense system, the U.S. launches a 120-pound "kill vehicle" that successfully intercepts a dummy warhead over the Pacific.

Oct. 5 A Bank of New York employee and two others are indicted on charges of conspiring to transfer and receive almost $7 billion in unauthorized funds. All are Russian-born, although two had become U.S. citizens.

Oct. 13 Although most Democrats back it, the Senate shoots down the 1996 Comprehensive Test Ban Treaty, which prohibits nuclear weapons testing. The vote marks the first time in nearly 80 years that the Senate has rejected an international treaty.

Oct. 13 Despite 13 months of investigation into the 1996 murder case of six-year-old beauty queen Jon Benet Ramsey, a grand jury finds insufficient evidence to issue any indictments. The case remains open and unsolved.

Big Wheel

Behold the London skyline: Wee Ben (near left) and the diminutive Houses of Parliament. Or so the city's landmarks seem, now that an "observation wheel" called the London Eye looms above them. The millennial attraction (here, making its way toward a fully upright position), dreamed up by a husband-and-wife architect team and financed in part by British Airways, rises 450 feet—the city's fourth-highest structure. Each enclosed cabin holds up to 25 people; rotations last a leisurely half hour. On a clear day, riders can soak up vistas of 25 miles. On a rainy, foggy day . . . no problem, the weather's always perfect in London.

Déjà Vu

Islamic militants in Chechnya and Russian soldiers were at war again—after just three years. Amid reports of escalating civilian deaths, the separatist republic began hemorrhaging human beings: More than half of its population fled. Some 230,000, mostly women and children, flooded the neighboring republic of Ingushetia; nearly 4,000 scrambled across a mountainous—and frequently bombed—cattle path to cross into Georgia. A mile short of that haven, a young widow (in pink jacket) from the besieged capital city of Grozny sent her three-year-old son across the Argun River in the arms of a rebel guide, then let the guide carry her across the wet, wobbly logs. Her husband died in the last war, she said; she did not want her little boy to witness this one.

Oct. 14 Two days after ousting Pakistan's prime minister, the popular Gen. Pervez Musharraf promises to restore a democratic government eventually; he **declares himself leader,** dismisses Parliament and suspends the constitution.

Oct. 16 A 7.1-magnitude early morning earthquake—felt **from Los Angeles to Las Vegas**—strikes the Southern California desert, causing minor injuries.

Oct. 20 A two-year, Pentagon-funded study finds that an anti-nerve-gas drug given to some 250,000 U.S. troops during the gulf war **"cannot be ruled out"** as the cause of veterans' chronic pain, nausea, memory loss and digestive problems.

Oct. 22 Scientists report the isolation of a long-elusive enzyme, beta-secretase, that spurs the development of **Alzheimer's disease.** The finding may allow researchers to develop drugs to slow or reverse the degenerative condition.

Look What I Found

The Siberian reindeer herder who dug the woolly mammoth tusks out of the tundra took them to the nearest town, Khatanga, to sell (the ivory trade is serious business in Siberia). But French adventurer Bernard Buigues (right) got to the tusks first and had the nomad lead him to the discovery site. There, radar revealed the almost entirely preserved carcass of a 20,000-year-old mammoth buried in the permafrost. Buigues's team cut a block around the giant and airlifted the 23-ton chunk by helicopter to Khatanga. Come spring, scientists will thaw the earth away with hairdryers and study the shaggy beast.

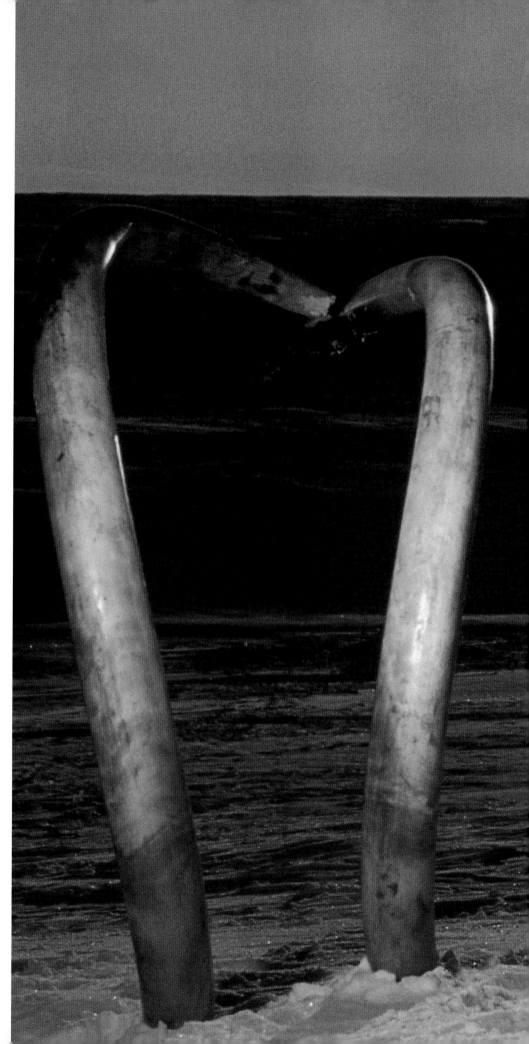

FRANCIS LATREILLE
CERPOLEX

Nov. 1 One of America's largest managed-care plans, UnitedHealthcare, becomes the first to ax a **widespread but much-criticized** provision requiring doctors to obtain insurance authorization prior to providing patient care.

Nov. 2 A Xerox employee, 40-year-old Bryan Uyesugi, who is suspected of having shot and **killed seven coworkers** at the company's Honolulu office hours earlier, surrenders to state authorities.

Nov. 3 In the nation's largest-ever environmental enforcement action, the U.S., acting on a two-year investigation by the EPA, **files lawsuits** against seven midwestern and southern electric utility companies, charging decades of illegal air pollution.

Nov. 4 Pharmaceutical giant Warner-Lambert agrees to a **$72 billion**, all-stock merger with American Home Products. If approved, the merger will create the largest pharmaceutical and consumer health products company in the world.

Lord of the Ring

Even his fans allowed that Evander Holyfield had been soundly bested by British boxer Lennox Lewis last March at Madison Square Garden—and that the judges' draw smacked of favoritism. But Holyfield loyalists hoped that when the two men met again in Las Vegas, the hard-hitting heavyweight, 37, who has a history of rematch triumphs, would hammer his way to a victory. Lewis backers banked on the 34-year-old's advantages in height, heft and age, and hoped that the cautious fighter would, as he had predicted, let go with a knockout punch. In the November rematch, the two men—whose few moments of all-out viciousness included Lewis's apparent effort to eject Holyfield from the ring (left)—danced for 12 rounds, after which the judges finally declared Lewis heavyweight champion of the world. "This," he said, "was my dream."

MIKE FIALA
AGENCE FRANCE PRESSE

Nov. 5 In his "findings of fact," U.S. District Judge Thomas Penfield Jackson declares that Microsoft **constitutes a monopoly** and has engaged in anticompetitive behavior.

Nov. 7 After eight 1999 wins, including four **consecutive championships,** Tiger Woods sets golf's new single-season earnings record: $6.6 million.

Nov. 10 American Egyptologists report the discovery of rock inscriptions created by Egyptians and Semitic-speaking peoples that may date the alphabet to **around 2000 B.C.**—three to four centuries earlier than was previously believed.

Nov. 12 President Clinton signs into law the Financial Services Modernization Act—**criticized by some** politicians for weak consumer privacy provisions—allowing banks, securities firms and insurers to merge and share information.

Aftermath

Survivors described clinging to trees to keep from being swept away by 160-mph winds or the thundering, 30-foot-high tidal wave. The supercyclone that struck the eastern coast was one of India's worst natural disasters in memory. At least 10,000 died (here, a journalist faces mud-caked corpses in Port Paradeep); 7.5 million were left homeless. What followed was a prolonged nightmare: Rotting corpses lay in the streets; contaminated drinking water brought cholera and typhoid; bungled local government relief efforts compounded the chaos. The emotional toll was immeasurable: Stunned villagers stood about like specters, testament to what one official called "a living hell."

RAGHU RAI
MAGNUM PHOTOS

Nov. 12 Three months after more than 17,000 perish in a powerful temblor, a **7.1-magnitude earthquake** strikes northwest Turkey. More than 750 are killed and 712 buildings toppled.

Nov. 15 Ending 13 years of on-and-off negotiations, American and Chinese leaders sign a **landmark trade agreement** that clears the way for China's entry into the World Trade Organization.

Nov. 16 A Michigan jury convicts Nathaniel Abraham—**one of the youngest** persons ever to be tried for a slaying—of second-degree murder for a crime committed when he was 11.

Nov. 29 More than a year after the Good Friday peace accord, the formation of a joint Protestant-Catholic government in Northern Ireland sets the stage for the **transfer of power** from London to Belfast.

Take a Gander

Go to Pamplona for the running of the bulls, but go to Mirano if you're dying to see—and who isn't?—the running of the geese. Traditionally, tenant farmers in this northern Italian village offered geese to landlords around November 11, the feast day of Saint Martin. Nowadays, come November, the entire village gets goose-happy: The bird shows up in dishes from antipasto to dessert, and the main piazza is transformed into a goose-themed board game. Ten years ago, a local restaurateur hatched the idea of a 500-yard "Palio of the Goose," in which trainers dress up as old-fashioned *paesani* and keep their birds from running afoul with light taps of switches. This year's winner, Lola (at left), speed-waddled to the finish in five minutes. Her 10-year-old trainer got a charity-bound cash prize and a basket of salami.

Nov. 30 Seattle Mayor Paul Schell calls in the National Guard to help control a small but **violent faction** of the 25,000 demonstrators outside a World Trade Organization meeting. To restore calm, Schell declares a curfew and a 50-square-block "no protest" zone.

Dec. 3 After 81 days (and 3,000 miles) at sea, lawyer Tori Murden, 36, becomes **the first American** and the first woman to row across the Atlantic Ocean solo.

Dec. 7 NASA officials are forced to conclude that a $165 million unmanned probe, Polar Lander, is **lost on the Red Planet.** Another Mars probe, the Climate Orbiter, disappeared in September.

Dec. 9 Pvt. Calvin Glover, 18, is sentenced to life in prison for beating Pfc. Barry Winchell, 21, a gay barracks mate, to death with a baseball bat. The trial revealed that antigay **harassment was commonplace** at Fort Campbell, Ky.

Terrible Tower

Witnesses described the thunderous crack that may have been the center pole snapping, then the roar of thousands of tumbling logs set up for a bonfire, and the screams of those trapped in the massive snarl of wood and wire. Eleven students and an alumnus were fatally crushed at Texas A&M's College Station campus while working on the symbol of their "burning desire" to beat the University of Texas in a Thanksgiving football game. Sophomore Tim Kerlee (top left), who fell from the 40-foot structure, directed rescue workers to other victims; he died a day later of internal injuries. Despite the ritual's dangers, most in the A&M family stoutly defended the 90-year tradition. "It's got to continue," said Kerlee's mother, Janice.

Dec. 9 The State Department orders the expulsion of Russian diplomat Stanislav Borisovich Grusev, who was arrested outside its Washington, D.C., headquarters while monitoring an **eavesdropping device** hidden in a conference room.

Dec. 10 Former Los Alamos physicist Wen Ho Lee is arrested on charges of security violations involving **American nuclear weapons.** He continues to deny giving any secrets to China.

Dec. 14 Former President Jimmy Carter represents the U.S. at ceremonies marking the official turnover of the **Panama Canal.** Panamanian sovereignty over Teddy Roosevelt's pet project takes effect at noon, December 31.

Dec. 21 Rescue efforts—and the evacuation of some of the **150,000 left homeless**—continue in the wake of devastating rain-triggered mudslides in Venezuela. The death toll will remain an estimate (more than 20,000), since the bodies of many who perished are buried under 20 feet of earth.

Stars Bright

There's nothing like gazing up at the stars to keep us down-to-earth. Although our millennium has been extraordinary—dizzying—this composite photograph by the Hubble Space Telescope, of two galaxies destined to dance together before merging in another, oh, few billion years, reminds us that the past thousand years is barely a cosmic blink. We needn't feel diminished, however: We too have a place, if a mysterious one. "You and I are flesh and blood," said Helena Curtis, noted biology writer, "but we are also stardust." We share our very atoms with what is unimaginably far away.

NASA AND THE HUBBLE HERITAGE TEAM AURA/STSCI

"[Elizabeth Dole] has extended women's political history . . . simply by Being. Being a serious candidate."

Robin Givhan, *Washington Post* **writer**

"I had a lot of things I was going to do when I became the first First Man."

Bob Dole, following his wife's withdrawal from the presidential race

Happy New Year!
The world did not end on December 31, 1999. How come? One possibility: Experts agree that the next calendar millennium doesn't begin until January 1, 2001. Another: That the second millennium has already arrived, unnoticed; historical recalculations have led some experts to date Jesus' birth as early as 7 "B.C."

THE POWER OF PINK

Barbra Streisand cleaned out her closets, and our wallets, at Christie's auctions. Total take: nearly $5 million.

Toy story

Worldwide, they've sold about $7 billion in merchandise. Kids are crazy for Pokémon. Should parents try to catch up with the names of more than 150 "pocket monsters," the computer games, the trading cards, the cartoon and the new movie? Maybe not. Wrote one mom who probed her nine-year-old daughter's obsession: "What she really loves is that I have no clue what she's talking about."

FLASHBACK: TURN OF TWO CENTURIES

	1899	1999
Median age of U.S. population	23	36
Percent of the population that is 65 and older	4	13

We love them, don't we?

Perhaps hoping to further spur the acquisitive impulse in young'uns, the U.S.P.S. chose National Stamp Collecting Month, October, to highlight something else that kids have always loved to gather. And the stamps are perforated, just like jar lids.

"[Attorney General John] Mitchell was arguing strenuously about the law this morning, and I said, 'Goddammit, forget the law.'"
President Richard Nixon, in tapes released this year

Yes, sir, that's our baby

On December 1, at the age of 102 (days), the San Diego Zoo's panda cub was formally named Hua Mei, meaning "China U.S.A." or "Splendid Beauty." The miracle baby—four ounces at birth—captivated us via 24-hour-a-day "Panda Cam" on the Internet.

"I mean, here we are, in what is supposed to be the happiest, mellowest city on the planet, and look what's happening."

Seattle native Charles Rowin, on anti–World Trade Organization protests that tore his city apart in December

---

Tell the kids I love them.

—God

You might want to pay attention

If I were a Carpenter...

It was just a pick-me-up for TV's summer doldrums—but it wouldn't go away. After ratings soared (seven of the top 10 slots in one November week) and IRS employee John Carpenter hit the jackpot, *Who Wants to Be a Millionaire* was added to ABC's regular 2000 schedule. Host Regis Philbin (above) was happy. As were viewers: One academic called the show the "programming equivalent of crack cocaine."

"She was just born a nice, quiet little kiddo."

Jenna Welch, 80, on daughter Laura (Mrs. George W.) Bush's calming effect on her husband

---

Field day

The Splendid Splinter, Ted Williams, gave us the wave twice this year: at Boston's All-Star game and at Atlanta's honoring of the All-Century Team (here, with Hank Aaron and Willie Mays). He was the icing on a cake of a season. The homer count was high and included a grand slam—if he had made it around the bases—by the Mets' Robin Ventura, to end the most exciting playoff game in memory. The Yankees swept the World Series. And Red Sox pitcher Pedro Martínez took the A.L. Cy Young Award—unanimously.

Say "cheese!"

Artist Spencer Tunick says it's easy to find people to bare all for shots like this New York City one, so he's aiming even higher. Someday: 2,000 nudies in Central Park!

TIME & AGAIN

One way to brace for a new century is to examine the old one, i
Herewith, a brief visit to some high and low points of the on

10 YEARS AGO

The image will never go away: One heroic protester (fate unknown) facing a row of tanks in Beijing's Tiananmen Square.

The Berlin Wall crumbled, a potent symbol of the new freedom sweeping Eastern Europe.

Oil tanker *Exxon Valdez* hit a reef, spilling 11 million gallons of crude and fouling 1,000 miles of shoreline.

30 YEARS AGO

50 YEARS AGO

60 YEARS AGO

The world shared the suspense as Americans (here, Buzz Aldrin photographed by Neil Armstrong) set foot on the moon.

Clayton Moore and Jay Silverheels brought the Lone Ranger and Tonto to vivid life on the small screen.

On August 31, the Führer ordered his troops to invade Poland. Within days, England and France had declared war on the Reich.

moments both large and small.
hundred years we call our own.

20 YEARS AGO

It was a nuclear nightmare from which the industry may never recover: Seven years before the Chernobyl disaster, a partial core meltdown at Pennsylvania's Three Mile Island power plant frightened thousands into fleeing the area.

Two young actresses made indelible marks: Judy Garland, 16, as Kansas's all-American Dorothy in *The Wizard of Oz* and Brit Vivien Leigh, 25, as the indomitable southern belle Scarlett O'Hara in *Gone with the Wind*.

Duke Ellington

Fred Astaire

Gloria Swanson

Humphrey Bogart

Alfred Hitchcock

Remembering

John F. Kennedy Jr.

His gifts were many: He was charismatic, generous, athletic and dashingly handsome. The gift he lacked: length of life. John F. Kennedy Jr. was 38 when the plane he was piloting crashed into the ocean waters off Martha's Vineyard on July 16, killing him, his wife, Carolyn, 33, and her sister Lauren Bessette, 34. Like his secret 1996 wedding, his death was a rare pivotal moment not captured in the media spotlight. Everything he did fascinated the world. Why? Perhaps because despite losing his father (the President) and beloved uncle (RFK) to assassins' bullets, despite growing up amid the privileges and perils of his famously infamous family, and despite being a living icon—and the son of two icons— he was amazingly well adjusted and robustly enthusiastic about life. His failures may have made him the butt of jokes (THE HUNK FLUNKS), and his flings (Daryl Hannah) and foibles (the struggling *George*) tabloid fodder, but he made a nation that watched him grow to manhood proud. Would he have carried the torch? When asked by friends about his political ambitions, he would smile and say, "Not in this century." No one expected that the truth would be "never" and that he would join his mother, father and uncle as a Kennedy who will forever be mourned.

Mel Tormé

His first gig, at a Chicago club, was a limited run: The kid had to start kindergarten in the fall. By nine he was a successful performer on radio serials, and by 21 he was the Velvet Fog, a bobby-sox singing sensation. But he soon grew impatient with his own "light, creamy, callow" crooning and adopted a freer, jazz-flavored style. His supple baritone could caress a song or take on the swingingest scat. He was also an accomplished drummer, actor, arranger and a prolific composer. "I'm still learning how to sing, how to stretch out," he said in the '80s, long after he had become a national treasure. His voice was stilled by a stroke in 1996; he died this year at 73.

James Farmer

After Farmer and a white friend were thrown out of a Chicago coffee shop in 1942, the pair and their supporters staged a sit-in. It was the birth of the Congress of Racial Equality—and civil rights activism (including the Freedom Rides) that led to many jail stints for Farmer. He was behind bars in August 1963 when Dr. Martin Luther King Jr. made his I Have a Dream speech at the March on Washington. Farmer, who died in July at 79, sent his own speech, which was read by an aide. "We will not stop," he wrote, "till the dogs stop biting us in the South and the rats stop biting us in the North."

Yehudi Menuhin

At his 1927 Carnegie Hall debut, Yehudi Menuhin's fingers were still too small to tune his violin. Few child prodigies have matched the musical maturity of the 11-year-old New York–born son of Russian immigrants; fewer still have equaled Menuhin's staying power: The purity of his tone and the depth of his interpretations thrilled audiences for seven decades. Menuhin, who died in March at 82, dabbled in jazz and Indian music, practiced yoga, crusaded for world peace. The former prodigy was also a tireless champion of musically talented young people. To the end, he kept his childlike aura—and the genius that once moved Albert Einstein to embrace him and exclaim, "Now I know there is a God in heaven."

Joe DiMaggio

From Ernest Hemingway's *The Old Man and the Sea:* "'I would like to take the great DiMaggio fishing,' the old man said. 'They say his father was a fisherman. Maybe he was as poor as we are and would understand.'" Born in 1914, one of nine children of Sicilian immigrants, maybe DiMaggio would have understood. We'll never know, for he was as enigmatic as he was charismatic. Through his nine World Series championships, his 56-game hitting streak of 1941, through his 274-day marriage to Marilyn Monroe, he remained private. We claim him anyway. For us, as for Hemingway, he is a touchstone: a ballplayer, a hero.

SPORTING NEWS-ARCHIVE PHOTOS

Wilt Chamberlain

He understood the problem: "Nobody loves Goliath." And so Wilt
Chamberlain was, perhaps, the most misunderstood athlete of the
century. A goateed black man more than seven feet tall who could
score by throwing the ball down rather than up—he once made
100 points in a single game—was an intimidating figure. But off
the court, and in his soul, he was a gentle man. He and Boston
Celtic center Bill Russell waged epic battles around the rim but
then broke bread at Wilt's house on Thanksgiving. Russell
remembered Chamberlain's curiosity and intelligence when he died
at 63. "As far as I'm concerned, he and I will be friends through
eternity." Not everyone misunderstood Wilt Chamberlain.

Lili St. Cyr

She was born Willis Marie Van Schaack but known as Lili St. Cyr: burlesque pioneer, striptease artist, model for a generation of sex symbols. Famed in the 1940s and '50s for her whispery voice and onstage bubble baths, Lili, who died at age 80, made a career out of being haughty and mysterious. The archetypal blonde bombshell (she married six times) was said to have inspired one young actress to dye her hair, don a sexy dress and turn herself into Marilyn Monroe.

Charles Pierce

He strutted the stage in clouds of boas and finger-length false eyelashes and sequined gowns. He told campy, wicked jokes: "I feel like a million," his Mae West drawled, "but I'll take them 10 at a time." His impersonations of screen divas didn't depend on costumes, makeup or one-liners, however. Pierce had trained as an actor. He didn't do Dietrich and Swanson and Streisand so much as become them, capturing their every gesture and facial expression. He tried to hang up his gowns for good in the '80s, but after the 1989 death of Bette Davis, his fans demanded he bring back his signature character. Fasten Your Seat Belts was the doyen of drag's last tour. He died at 72.

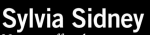
Sylvia Sidney

No one suffered onscreen more soulfully. In films throughout the '30s, Sylvia Sidney played a valiant working girl victimized by bad men or bad luck. Her sad saucer eyes and wounded quality won her critical praise, most notably in *Dead End, An American Tragedy* and *Street Scene.* In real life, Sidney suffered less sweetly. She threw hair-raising tantrums on the set and groused, with good reason, about being typecast. "They always had me ironing somebody's shirt," she would recall. As film work thinned, the actress found more varied parts onstage—in roles from Auntie Mame to Anne Boleyn—and on television. With her Oscar-nominated performance in 1973's *Summer Wishes, Winter Dreams,* Sidney returned to movies; her last role before her death at 88 was the dotty grandmother in Tim Burton's *Mars Attacks!* "Being a movie star never meant much to me," she once said, "but being an actress did."

George C. Scott

George Campbell Scott was one of the great American actors of the last half century: intuitive, artful, explosive. Yet, in the end, audiences did not quite get their due. He had a handful of indelible stage performances (Richard III, Willy Loman, Shylock) but never essayed Lear, for example. He bequeathed a mere half-dozen worthy films: *Anatomy of a Murder, The Hustler, Dr. Strangelove, Petulia, The Hospital* and, of course, *Patton.* Scott was born in 1927 in a Virginia mining town; his family soon relocated to Detroit. After four noncombat years in the Marines, where he embraced boozing, he entered college and was hooked by acting. Those twin compulsions would define him, rendering a life scorched by demons but salved by integrity (he spurned awards, calling the Oscars a "meat parade"). He married five times, actresses all.

Payne Stewart

The man with the smoothest, silkiest swing in the game of golf was, a year before his death in a freak airplane crash, riding a seven-season slump. His reputation was left over from his bygone time in the spotlight: a talented but difficult man, full of himself. But Stewart enjoyed a marvelous renaissance as an athlete in 1999, winning the U.S. Open a second time and taking part in his country's victorious Ryder Cup campaign. Fans learned that he was a changed man. He had found faith and peace of mind; his colleagues said he had become one of the most generous, affable guys in the game. What happened to 42-year-old Payne Stewart was tragic, certainly, but not as tragic as it would have been had it happened at an earlier time.

Dusty Springfield

She started life as an English convent schoolgirl named Mary Isabel Catherine O'Brien, but by 11 she was already transforming herself into Dusty, scandalizing the nuns with a raunchy "St. Louis Blues" at the school talent show. She grew to become both the undisputed Queen of British soul ("Son of a Preacher Man") and a matchless interpreter of pop standards (Burt Bacharach's "Wishin' and Hopin'"). On the surface, her style was gaudy: She wore huge raccoonlike circles of eye makeup and hairdos that she said required "so much hairspray, I feel personally responsible for global warming." But she was a profoundly serious person (she was deported from South Africa in 1964 for insisting on integrated audiences) and an artist so meticulous that she sometimes recorded one syllable at a time. When producer Jerry Wexler presented her with 75 songs to choose for an album, "she liked exactly zero." The end product, *Dusty in Memphis*, became a classic, but Dusty was never satisfied. The rest of the world was: Her death at 59, from breast cancer, came 13 days before her induction into the Rock and Roll Hall of Fame.

Walter Payton

It surprised some casual observers of the game that the player being mourned, Walter Payton, was, in fact, the top rusher in the history of the National Football League. They might have bet on elegant, elusive Gale Sayers, bruiser Jim Brown or even, yes, O.J. Simpson. But in 13 seasons with the Chicago Bears, from 1975 through 1987, Payton, who could do it all—catch, block, break a tackle, break a long one—gained 16,726 yards, more than anyone ever. However, neither his NFL title (he and the Bears won the '86 Super Bowl) nor his rushing record should be considered the proper legacy of this man who died much too young, at 45, of a rare liver ailment. Sweetness, as Payton was called, was drafted by the Bears when he was only 20. He had already earned his bachelor's degree and was working on a master's in education for the deaf, not because he suspected he might not make it in football but "to help dispel the myth that athletes in general and black athletes in particular don't have to work to get their diplomas and that they don't learn anything anyway."

Pee Wee Reese

Harold Henry Reese couldn't shake the nickname he had earned as a kid in
Louisville, Ky. (by winning a marbles competition with his "peewee" shooter),
but he grew up to be very big indeed. The shortstop's unshakable support of
his black teammate eased Jackie Robinson's transition during that wrenching
1947 season, when major league baseball's color barrier was broken. "It was his
friendship and understanding that carried me over the tough spots," Robinson
said. After leading two generations of Dodgers to seven pennants, it was fitting
that Reese made the final putout of the 1955 World Series, as the Dodgers
snapped their five-Series losing streak against the Yankees. The Little Colonel
had never fully retired from the game when he died at 81, having soldiered on as
a Dodgers coach, baseball announcer and representative for Louisville Sluggers.

Joe Williams

In the late '40s he spent a year in a hospital for depression. Afterward, he hawked cosmetics door-to-door in Chicago until he could make a living from his music. Finally, in 1955, Joe Williams scored his first hit. Fronting Count Basie's band, he delivered the hard-driving "Everyday (I Have the Blues)" with a smooth, urbane elegance that marked him, finally, as a jazz master. He and Basie made swinging music together for five more years; with the Count and later as a solo he fine-tuned his powerful baritone, stretching his repertoire to ballads, up-tempo tunes, pop songs, spirituals, scat. He was a luminous, charming performer and a resolutely happy man. "I've tried desperately," he said, "to fend off any of the feelings that are going to mar my life." He died at 80 in Las Vegas.

Stanley Kubrick

His movies shocked, entertained, sparked protest and endeared him to cinephiles everywhere. A New Yorker who exiled himself to England, Stanley Kubrick directed just 13 features; several—*Dr. Strangelove, 2001: A Space Odyssey* and *A Clockwork Orange*—are hailed as masterworks. By his death at age 70, he had acquired a mythical stature, fueled by his perfectionism: To faithfully reproduce a 1700s ambience for *Barry Lyndon*, for example, he filmed by candlelight with a special lens. Kubrick so reliably challenged viewers that Janet Maslin, one of the few critics to admire his last film, *Eyes Wide Shut*, labeled his movies "irresistible intellectual catnip."

Victor Mature

"I can act," he told LIFE in 1941, "but what I've got that the others don't have is This." Then he pointed at his body. What a body: doorway-wide shoulders, weightlifter's chest, wavy ink-black hair, bedroom eyes. Men found him too luscious, women swooned: After his 1939 screen debut, which lasted all of five minutes, 20,000 fans sent mash notes. Only a handful of his 55 films were any good, but he was fine as the dying Doc Holliday in *My Darling Clementine* and as the muscle man in *Samson and Delilah*. He died at 86, having spent the last 40 years of his life golfing. Even in retirement, however, he couldn't resist the occasional role—usually playing a parody of his earlier self.

Saul Steinberg

His *New Yorker* drawings were often a stew of styles—sleek art deco skyscrapers kept company with Cubist abstractions and childish scrawls. And his work could be obscure, as could he (at left, he holds hands with his young self). "Psychiatrists," he said, "are lecherous about me." Romanian-born, he satirized America, sometimes harshly. But his most-reproduced image was a good-humored poke at Manhattan provincialism: Ninth and Tenth avenues eat up the foreground while America beyond the Hudson River is reduced to a forlorn strip. A week after his death at 84, *The New Yorker* ran Saul Steinberg's 86th cover.

Donald Mills

His father had his own barbershop quartet, so it was no surprise that Donald and his brothers began crooning their honeyed harmonies early in life. They made their professional debut in 1924; Donald, the youngest, was seven. By 1931 the Mills Brothers (clockwise, from top right: father John, who joined after his oldest son died of a lung ailment in 1936; Donald; Harry; Herbert) had their first hit—the jaunty "Tiger Rag" ("Hold that tiger!") featured their nifty trick of mimicking instruments. The first black group to be widely embraced by whites, they stayed on top of the charts with hits like "Paper Doll" and "Glow Worm." In the early '80s, Donald began singing with his son. "As long as I can walk onstage and have the audience sing along," the last surviving Mills brother said in 1997, "I'll be there."

Kim Perrot

"Put a challenge in front of her, and she'd fight you tooth and nail," said Houston Comets coach Van Chancellor. He had initially doubted that the five-foot-five dynamo had the skills—or stature—to succeed in the WNBA. But Kim Perrot, who paid her dues by playing abroad for six years before trying out for a slot stateside, proved him wrong. Her ferocious defensive style and fierce enthusiasm for the game earned her a spot as the Comets' starting point guard; she averaged 8.5 points and 4.7 assists, making 84 steals in her last regular season—and rallied her team to two back-to-back WNBA championships. But challenges off the court were insurmountable: The 32-year-old lost her six-month battle with cancer on the eve of her team's third playoff run.

BILL BAPTIST/WNBA PHOTOS

Harry Blackmun, 90

Looking back, it seems hardly possible that the celebrated and vilified author of *Roe* v. *Wade* was Nixon's "safe" choice for the Supreme Court, where he served for 24 years.

Anita Carter, 66

A scion of country music's founding family, the gifted soprano—and child radio star—performed with stars like the great Hank Snow, who died this year at 85.

Iron Eyes Cody, 94

After decades of playing Native Americans onscreen, the actor and activist achieved icon status when he shed a single tear in a memorable 1971 antipollution ad.

Pete Conrad, 69

The unflagging exuberance of the third person to walk on the moon impressed everyone, even Navy pilot colleagues—who acknowledged him as their twist dance champion.

SUZANNE DECHILLO/NYT PICTURES

Sarah Delany, 109

The quietly remarkable Delany sisters had their say in a best-selling oral history and an acclaimed Broadway play. Bessie, who died in 1995, was a dentist; Sadie, a home-ec teacher.

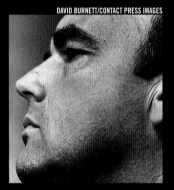

DAVID BURNETT/CONTACT PRESS IMAGES

John Ehrlichman, 73

The jut-jawed bully of the Watergate hearings never apologized for his crimes as Nixon's domestic policy adviser—but he did his time (18 months) without whining.

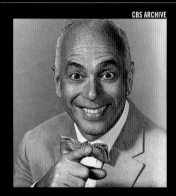

CBS ARCHIVE

Allen Funt, 84

With *Candid Camera*, the affable host (who swore that he wasn't a practical joker as a kid) became America's premier prankster—and set the stage for "caught-in-the-act" TV.

SUZANNE OPTON/BLACK STA

Joseph Heller, 76

Many have aspired to write the Great American Novel. With *Catch-22*, the dark and hilarious tour de force that sold 10 million copies, the kid from Coney Island succeeded.

FRANK CAPRI/ARCHIVE PHOTOS

Madeline Kahn, 57

Baby-voiced and irresistible, the comic actress won a Tony for her role in *The Sisters Rosensweig* and an Oscar nomination as the saloon singer in *Blazing Saddles*

TIMOTHY GREENFIELD-SANDERS/CORBIS OUTLINE

Oseola McCarty, 91

The Hattiesburg, Miss., washerwoman used $150,000 of her life savings to create a scholarship fund so deserving black students "won't have to work so hard, like I did."

ALICE OCHS/MICHAEL OCHS ARCHIVES

Shel Silverstein, 68

The best-selling author created a child's anarchic paradise where Ridiculous Rose ate with her toes, Captain Hook refrained from picking his nose and adults didn't stand a chance.

PHOTOFES

Señor Wences, 103

The ventriloquist who gave us the catchphrase "S'awright?" "S'awright!" was a frequent guest on *The Ed Sullivan Shou* and the object of exceptional respect among his colleagues

Index

Note: Page numbers
of photographs are in **bold** type.

A

Abraham, Nathaniel, 127

Agassi, Andre, 97

Ali, Laila, **75**

Alzheimer's disease, 120

American Airlines

    Flight 1420, **55**

    pilots, 16

Anthony, Marc, **37**

Armstrong, Lance, **107**

Arnaz, Desi, **38**

Ashbrook, Larry, 98

Ashby, Capt. Richard J., 19

Astaire, Fred, **137**

AT&T, 51

Avalanches, **16**

B

Backstreet Boys, **65**

Bakersfield (Calif.), **6**

Bank of New York, 117

Barak, Ehud, 55

Barbie, **30**

Barton, Mark, 85

Baseball, season opener, 43

    stadiums, 67

    umpires, 94

Belgrade protests, 90

Benigni, Roberto, **32**

Berlin, 90

Berlin Wall, **136**

Big Bird, **103**

Blackmun, Harry, **158**

Blair Witch Project, The **105**

Blue moon, 29

Bogart, Humphrey, **137**

Bregenz (Austria) opera, **80**

Breitling Orbiter 3, **23**

Brooklyn, Ohio, **65**

C

California earthquake, 120

Cape Hatteras Lighthouse, **62**

Carter, Anita, **158**

Castro, Fidel, **103**

Cézanne still life, **66**

Chamberlain, Wilt, **143**

Charles, Prince, **30**

Chastain, Brandi, **72**

Chechnya, refugees, **118**

Chicago cow show, **68**

China trade agreement, 127

Citadel, The, 55

City of New Orleans, **20**

Clemente, Roberto, **38**

Clinton, Bill, **29**, 85

Clinton, Hillary, **79**

Coca-Cola, 82

Cody, Iron Eyes, **158**

Colombia earthquake, **9**

Columbine High School, 40, **109**

Comprehensive Test Ban

    Treaty, 117

Computer virus, 43

Conrad, Pete, **158**

Cooper, Cynthia, **71**

Cruz, Celia, **38**

D

Dartmouth College, 13

Delany, Sarah, **158**

Diallo, Amadou, 13

DiMaggio, Joe, **142**

Dole, Elizabeth, **133**

Dolly, **29**

"Don't ask, don't tell," 10

Dow-Jones, 27

Dreamcast, **105**

E

East Timor, 93, 98

Eclipse, **93**

Edward, Prince, 52

Egypt, ancient alphabet, 124

    mummies, **90**

EgyptAir Flight 990, **114**

Ehrlichman, John, **158**

Ellington, Duke, **137**

Elway, John, **33**

Embryo mix-up, 47

EPA lawsuits, 123

Ethiopia, bone discovery, 47

Euro, 9

European Commission, 20

Exxon Valdez, **136**

F

Falun Gong, 48

Farmer, James, **140**

FBI and Waco, Tex., 90

Financial Services

    Modernization Act, 124

Florida wildfires, **43**

Ford Motor Co., 10

Frankel, Martin, 94

Fuentes, Daisy, **36**

Funt, Allen, **158**

Furrow, Buford O. Jr., **86**

G

Garland, Judy, **137**

Gates, Bill and Melinda, 98

Glover, Pvt. Calvin, 128

God (messages from), **31, 67,**

    105, 135

Gonzales, Pancho, **38**

Goose race, **127**

Gorbachev, Mikhail and Raisa, **97**

Graf, Steffi, **33**, 58

Greece, earthquake, 97

H

Gretzky, Wayne, **33**

Gulf war illness, 120

Hamm, Mia, **70**

Hand transplant, **13**

Harry Potter books, **104**

Hastert, Dennis, 9

Hazelwood, Joseph, 62

Heat wave, 85

Heller, Joseph, **158**

Henderson, Russell, 44

Hill, Lauryn, **31**

Hitchcock, Alfred, **137**

Holyfield, Evander, **123**

Honolulu slayings, 123

Hubbell, Webster, 62

Hubble Space Telescope, **131**

Hurricane Floyd, **98**

Hussein, King, 15

I

Iglesias, Julio, **38**

Impeachment trial, 9

Import limits, 79

Inca sacrifices, **66**

India, cyclone, **124**

Indonesia, election, **56**

Ireland, Patrick, **108–113**

J

Jenkins, Vincent, 93

Jenny Jones Show, The, 51

Johnson, Michael, **105**

Jones, Marion, **74**

Jordan, Michael, **33**

K

Kahn, Madeline, **158**

Kansas Board of Education, 86

Katzenberg, Jeffrey, 79

Kennedy, Carolyn Bessette, **139**

Kennedy, John F. Jr., **139**

Kevorkian, Dr. Jack, 23, **65**

King, John William, 16

Knievel, Robbie, 58

Kosovo, cease-fire, **58, 61**

    refugees, **4, 27, 44, 47**

Kubrick, Stanley, **154**

L

Latin explosion, **34–39**

Lee, Wen Ho, 19, 86, 131

Leigh, Vivien, **137**

Lemon Drop Kid, 61

Lewinsky, Monica, **19**

Lewis, Lennox, **123**

Lilly, Kristine, 73

London Eye, **117**

Lone Ranger and Tonto, **136**

Lopez, Jennifer, **39**

Lucci, Susan, **65**

M

Mallory, George, 51

Mars probe, 128

Martin, Ricky, **34**

Masters Tournament, 44

Mature, Victor, **155**

Mbeki, Thabo, 62

McCarty, Oseola, **158**

Menuhin, Yehudi, **140**

Mercury capsule, 48

Microsoft, 124

Millennium, 133

Mills, Donald, **156**

Mir, 93

Missile defense system, 117

Monarch butterfly, **67**

Moon landing, **136**

Moreno, Rita, **38**

Murden, Tori, 128

Mustang Ranch, **106**

N

National Basketball Assoc., 13

NATO, air strikes, 23, **24,** 55

    anniversary, 47

    helicopter rescue, 23

    new members, 19

NCAA men's championship, 27

NCAA women's championship, 27

New Carissa, **10**

Niger, assassination, 44

Nigeria, election, 16

Noor, Queen, **15**

Northern Ireland, 127

Nuclear accident, Japan, 98

Nunavut, 43

O

Oklahoma tornado, **51**

Olympic Committee,

    International, 20

Oscars-gown auction, **67**

P

Pakistan coup, 120

Paltrow, Gwyneth, 29

Pan Am Flight 103, 44

Panama Canal, 131

Panda cub, **134**

Payton, Walter, **150**

Perrot, Kim, **157**

Phantom Menace, The, **66**

Pierce, Charles, **145**

Pokémon, **134**

Pope John Paul II, 10, **61**

Puente, Tito, **38**

Q

Queen Mother, the, 86

R

Racial profiling, 47

Ramsey, Jon Benet, 117

Reese, Pee Wee, **151**

Resendez-Ramirez, Rafael, 82

Rhys-Jones, Sophie, **52**

Rivera, Chita, **38**

Robotic dog, **104**

RollerJam, **32**

Ryder Cup, **104**

S

St. Cyr, Lili, **144**

Salinger, J.D., **67**

Salt Lake City tornado, **88**

Santana, Carlos, **38**

Saxetenbach Gorge, 85

Scott, George C., **147**

Scurry, Briana, **72**

Sheindlin, Judge Judy, **31**

Sidney, Sylvia, **146**

Silverstein, Shel, **158**

Sixth Sense, The, **105**

Soliah, Kathleen Ann, 61

Solomon, Thomas, 58

Sonic boom, **76**

Sow, Ousmane, **32**

Springfield, Dusty, **149**

Spying, Russian, 131

Stayner, Cary, 82

Steinberg, Saul, **156**

Stewart, Payne, **148**

Streisand, Barbra, **133**

Swanson, Gloria, **137**

T

Taiwan earthquake, **100**

Talic, Gen. Momir, 90

Tehran protests, 79

Texas A&M bonfire, **128**

Thompson, Jenny, **72**

Three Mile Island, **137**

Tiananmen Square, **136**

Tobacco lawsuits, 27, 79

Tormé, Mel, **140**

Tunick, Spencer, **135**

Turkey, earthquake, **94,** 127

Twain, Shania, **103**

Typhoon Olga, **85**

U

Uganda, kidnapping, 16

UnitedHealthcare, 123

U.S. Dept. of Agriculture, 9

U.S. Mint, **31**

U.S. Navy enlistment, 10

U.S.P.S. stamps, **30, 67, 106, 134**

U.S. soldiers released by Serbia, 48

V

Venezuela, mudslides, 131

Vernoff, Gaby, 20

Viacom-CBS merger, 97

Volpe, Justin, 58

W

Warner-Lambert, 123

Waterman, Vickie, **74**

Wences, Señor, **158**

Whale hunt, **48**

Who Wants to Be a

    Millionaire, **135**

Williams, Joe, **153**

Williams, Serena, **72,** 97

Williams, Ted, **135**

Women athletes, **70–75**

Woods, Tiger, 124

Woodstock '99, **82**

Woolly mammoth, **120**

World Trade Organization, 128

World War II, **136**

Y

Yeltsin, Boris, 55